The Soul of Adolescence

The Soul *of* Adolescence

In Their Own Words

PATRICIA LYONS

Morehouse Publishing
NEW YORK · HARRISBURG · DENVER

Morehouse Publishing, 4775 Linglestown Road, Harrisburg, PA 17112
Morehouse Publishing, 445 Fifth Avenue, New York, NY 10016
Morehouse Publishing is an imprint of Church Publishing Incorporated.

Cover image courtesy of Digital Vision / Jupiterimages
Cover design by Laurie Klein Westhafer
Typeset by Vicki K. Black

Library of Congress Cataloging-in-Publication Data
Lyons, Patricia.
The soul of adolescence: in their own words / Patricia Lyons.
        p.   cm.
Includes bibliographical references.
ISBN 978-0-8192-2375-3 (pbk.)
1. Teenagers—Religious life. 2. Teenagers—Attitudes. 3. Soul—Public opinion. I. Title.
BL625.47.L86 2010
200.835—dc22
                                            2009049599
Printed in the United States of America

10 11 12 13 14 15   10 9 8 7 6 5 4 3 2 1

CONTENTS

*This book is dedicated to
my mother*

LORNA LYONS

*my best friend, my shepherd,
and my Giving Tree*

ACKNOWLEDGMENTS

According to Webster's dictionary, a *midwife* is not only a person who assists in the miracle of literal birth, but also a person who is present and active "in the creation of new things or new life." It would take the length of a book to name all the midwives in my journey to giving birth to this book. I am in grateful awe of the company of souls who have spent time walking—some for days, some for decades—alongside me since childhood. This book is my attempt to shape and sculpt just some the unmerited clay given to me by the loving and wise hands and hearts of others. This book is ours, not mine.

There would never have been a book without the wise and joyful mentoring of the Reverend Dr. Roger Ferlo. Since the death of my own father when I was a teenager, I have been in awe of the strong spiritual fathers that God has shared with me in a constant and compassionate procession of parental and priestly love. Father Ferlo is a cross-bearer in this cloud of witnesses, and it was he who insisted on being the matchmaker between me and my gifted editor at Church Publishing, Cynthia Shattuck, whose skilled soul so often healed my struggling words and whose spirit tugged me toward forms of expression that matched the depth of my passion.

I also have so much gratefulness in my heart for the inspiration and love of my dear friend Dr. Lisa Kimball. Her faithful practice of showing up, listening, and telling the truth in my life has built a bridge into my heart for God to enter and empty every tomb in my soul.

My mentors at Harvard were numerous, but each played a role in setting small fires of passion for teaching, learning, and service of God and the church. My first friend among professors, Dr. Robert Coles, was both my teacher and my lifeline in the first semester of my college years. Father J. Bryan Hehir entrusted me to teach children in his church, but also embodied for me what it means to embrace and engage even the oldest of religious traditions and to take up love for that tradition as a beloved spouse. Dr. Courtney Bickel Lamberth taught me how and why to write, but more importantly modeled that good writing is an act of bravery and love. And the Reverend Professor Peter Gomes was and remains a beacon of hope, vocation, and faith for me and for literally tens of thousands of his students and colleagues. He is an image of the great Quaker command to "Let your life speak."

Fred, Mary Buford, and Eliza Hitz were and remain my first and most supportive spiritual family upon my entrance to the Episcopal Church. Their support of and commitment to my finding and using my gifts allowed me to envision and embark on a career in the classroom and the church without fear or hesitation. I am also grateful to Joan G. O. Holden, Head of St. Stephen's & St. Agnes School, whose faith in me and whose commitment to integrity and compassion stand as a lighthouse of loving leadership.

I thank Dr. Julianne Thomas, D.O., whose brave life commitment to the healing ministry of medicine has inspired me to seek the face, hear the voice, and experience the presence of God in the physical body of every human person, including myself. So much of her wisdom from the practice of medicine is contained in these pages. I thank my family and the many friends and colleagues who have held me up in prayer and fellowship. And I thank God for his unconditional love that has embraced and redeemed me through all things seen and unseen.

 *Introduction*

GRAFFITI
OF THE SOUL

For the last decade I have been on a search to understand what teenagers think and feel about the soul. There have been so many once-in-a-lifetime events in our country since I started this project that it feels like a bumpy and wild safari. My research started in the first decade of a new century that began in fear over whether or not the computers that are the veins of our lives would experience a Y2K meltdown. Since then, teenagers along with the rest of us have experienced a presidential election too close to call, a "titanic" terrorist attack on our soil, check points at every airport and large or symbolic public event, two wars pulling young people out of our classrooms and neighborhoods—some never to return, pictures of torture and abuse at the hands of Americans in uniform, the election of our first black president, and the near collapse of a global financial system once thought "too big to fail."

Over that time I took the opportunity to talk to as many different kinds of teenagers as possible. My venues for long surveys, extended conversations, and recorded interviews have included the formal setting of my classrooms in public and private high schools as a teacher of varied subjects, from advanced placement history to religion and ethics. But I have also talked with teens at conferences, on airplanes, Amtrak trains, and school buses. My conversations about the soul and the world have happened over meals, community service trips, youth conferences, international learning tours, and religious retreats. Whether I get a minute or an hour on my visits to schools, athletic fields, churches, or temples, I always ask teenagers my favorite question: *What is your definition of the soul?*

I have surveyed at length every student I have ever taught, piling up thousands of pages of writing (and doodling) from students of every race, class, economic background, and family situation. Whenever I tell young people that I have a personal life-project to gather adolescent definitions of the soul, teens who start out as complete strangers to me pour forth their ideas about the soul as if we'd been friends for years. I have collected crates of napkins, strips of newspapers, dog-eared maps, or other scrap paper that contain words about the soul from teenagers I have met on trips around America. Many students have given up on finding words for their definitions of the soul and instead have drawn me pictures or cartoons. Some have even folded papers into 3-D depictions of the soul. I have kept them all.

I have interviewed students at all types of schools: day schools and boarding schools, schools that are public, parochial, and private. I have interviewed foster children and adopted teens. I have brought pen and paper into drug rehabilitation centers and adolescent psychiatric wards and homeless shelters. I have interviewed first-generation American citizens in school bussing programs in public schools in Massachusetts as well as students at the nation's most elite private schools and colleges. I have held interviews with a broad spectrum of young people—schoolchildren in Honduras, affluent teenagers attending Oxford and Cambridge, Native Americans born in poverty on American Indian reservations, teenage runaways outside Atlantic City, and students in evangelical megachurches in California. I have discussed the soul with Mormon missionary teens in Salt Lake City, Jewish students after Shabbat services, student leaders of Sikh communities at colleges and universities, and Muslim volunteer groups about the concept of the soul in the Qur'an and in their own lives. While on residential Habitat for Humanity projects, I have asked teens to define the soul while they hung drywall or shingled a roof.

Whenever I can, I ask students for words, pictures, or music lyrics to help me understand their views of life, the world, and the soul. More than anything, I have learned that I could spend many more decades trying to understand better all the words I have gathered and what these words say about adolescents and about the adults in their lives. But there are trends of truth that have emerged clearly and beautifully—so much so that I have decided to stop, take stock, and share some of what I have heard so far about the soul of the adolescent.

The state of the soul of adolescents in America is not strong. We cannot have rational or helpful conversations and solutions for the emotional, social, or spiritual lives of teens until we admit that whatever we are doing in our homes, schools, youth clubs, or religious organizations right now is not producing a generation of young people with healthy habits of mind, body, and soul. If you believe we are currently succeeding in raising happy and healthy teens, even marginally, then you may be surprised and even taken aback by what young people are actually saying. If you do not believe that we are in fact at a crisis point with teenagers in this country, then this book may be the beginning of a new understanding of where young people are today.

Perhaps you are just not sure whether or not teens in this country are in trouble, and whether the troubles are getting worse. If so, please consider these truths on the ground.

- Despite the heroic efforts to combat youth smoking, a thousand kids start smoking every day.

- According to a U.S. Teen Sexual Activity study done by the Kaiser Family Foundation, 62 percent of teens have sexual experiences in high school—33 percent by the ninth grade. Sexually transmitted diseases are on the rise in every race and every economic class of young person, in all communities—rural, suburban, or urban.

- The use of crystal meth, an illegal drug proving more destructive by the day and one that was unheard of only a decade ago, is an epidemic in even the most rural and small-town neighborhoods of so-called middle America.

Increasing direct pharmaceutical advertising and the resulting parental demand for pills to relieve every adolescent issue from acne to depression have prompted a rise in the number of prescriptions, hovering around twenty times the number *per capita* than it was a generation ago. And unlike prior generations, more kids get their drugs from their own medicine cabinets these days than from any stranger on the street.

◆ Dating violence is on the rise, to the point of sparking a national debate and a push for legislation to protect teenagers from their own partners.

◆ Stories of the rise of cutting and other forms of self-mutilation regularly haunt the covers of major magazines; this secretive practice is hard to document, though some specialists put the number as high as one in ten young people.

◆ The third leading cause of death among teens, behind injury and disease, remains suicide, and, perhaps even more disturbing, it is the fifth leading cause of death of children aged ten to fourteen.

◆ According to a Center for Disease Control Youth Risk Behavior Surveillance Survey in 2005, in any given month 28.5 percent of high school students report one or more rides in a car with alcohol consumption present.

◆ According to the Ethics of American Youth study in 2008 conducted by the Josephson Institute, 40 percent of students report shoplifting and over half report stealing in high school. And those students who have abandoned school remind us we are making no progress in bringing down the nearly 48 percent high school dropout rate in this country.

In case you feel like you already know which kids are struggling with their moral and spiritual lives, and you feel sure that your child or student is not involved in such high-risk behaviors, consider a few more numbers: According to a landmark 2009 study, 86 percent of high school students report lying to teachers and parents and 80 percent report cheating every year in school, including four out of five National Merit Scholars.

Is the troubled teen still a stranger to you? When talking about adolescents we do well to remember the late Senator Daniel Patrick Moynihan's statement: "We are all entitled to our own opinions, but we are not entitled to our own facts." The fact is that whatever we are doing to support and mentor our teenagers in their moral and spiritual lives is not working. The beginning of any rational consideration of the problems and possible solutions requires that we admit this fact.

I am writing to the parent, the grandparent, the godparent, the teacher, the cleric, or the coach who is not sure exactly what to do to help our teens, but who knows that what we are doing is not working. And I am appealing to the adult who has a deep suspicion about the expectation that a taller trophy, a longer standardized test, or more expensive pieces of technology will solve or even address the ill soul of the adolescent. This book is for the adult who knows that simply doing more of what we are already doing, saying, buying, planning, or punishing is not going to make teens happier or healthier. I am writing to the loving mentors of adolescent lives who have a strong sense that we need a more spiritual script of new messages, new methods, and new metaphors. Adolescents will not listen to adults whose grown-up language is chiefly laced with adult reasoning, warnings, rewards, and punishments. Despite all our efforts at addressing the needs of teenagers, if we speak in a language based only on the grammar of our ideas and not theirs, teens will walk away. And who can blame them? How much could *you* learn from a wise man who speaks Farsi?

 *Chapter One*

THE BLACK
BOX SOUL

*"A soul is your true self—all that you are,
all that you keep hidden, all that you show the world."*

My older sister Linda spent the years before her early death drifting. Her life was marked by all the frustrating inconsistencies of so many teenagers in middle-class America. Like a rock in water, she maintained a constitutional resistance to the rich resources of love and adult presence around her. Once she became a teenager, she acted like an orphan, although she had loving parents; she acted like a refugee, although there was always a place for her to call home. She made decisions out of a palpable sense of insatiable neediness, although all of her physical needs were met. She struggled daily with social and emotional chaos of her own making; intellectually gifted, she performed far below her natural abilities in high school. She seemed unable to find a comfortable role for herself in the world, despite her family's relative stability both in the home and in the community. Both my parents worked from our home and were available for her at virtually any time. My mother was a Girl Scout leader; my father was a member of Rotary. My sister knew where to find all the adults in her life—she just did not appear to want to.

I know my sister's early years only through a dozen or so photographs that portray a busy childhood of Girl Scouting, youth athletic leagues, birthday parties, and religious celebrations. My mother was nineteen when Linda was born in the first year of her marriage. My father was a young war veteran just back from Korea. In photographs of their first decade as a family, the three of them look like a trio of friends, attending the World's Fair in New York in 1967 or a dude ranch the following year. However, almost to the day that my sister became a teenager, the climate of our house changed forever. My mother used to say that Linda went from making brownies with her to staying out all night with strangers. Her teen years began a cycle of making and then barely escaping the destructive choices of smoking, drinking, drugs, sex, and risky boyfriends on motorcycles. One sign of our family's state of crisis is that I do not have a single Kodak picture from that period, just the memory of an older sibling at war with her two young parents, a teenager whose strangely secretive and defensive personality felt like an alien in our home. Linda was twelve when my brother was born; fourteen when I arrived. This meant that my brother and I spent our childhoods sitting at the top of the stairs listening to the yelling that punctuated Linda's nearly decade-long war against my parents, the world, and herself.

In the calming twilight of those turbulent teen years, as she approached twenty-one, Linda began to come out of the fog of her adolescence. Many parents have watched their teenagers make this long-awaited transition, and my parents were as happy as any to see the impossible happening slowly before their eyes. My sister never got her act together to apply to college and therefore spent the years after high school living intermittently at home or with friends, working random jobs, and trying to find her footing. But although this young woman who had so many times come close to death in her adolescence appeared to be settling down, she tragically revisited her old habits one night, downing two drinks in one bar before driving to find an old boyfriend in another. That night she never arrived at the second destination.

Ironically, compared to the countless disastrous choices of her teen years, this choice to have two drinks and drive a few miles across town seems almost minor. Two state troopers, who slowly removed their hats at the sight of my parents for whom they had been looking all night, delivered the news that although my sister had somehow survived her disastrous adolescence, her single choice to drive while intoxicated the night before had ended her chance of living any longer. That picture of police officers ruining my parents' lives with just a handful of words is burned in my brain, and it has branded my life with a constant searching for the reasons behind my sister's inability to find meaning in her life and a stable sense of self. She did not die as a teenager, but she died as a result of the habits formed in her adolescence. While she was alive, her teenage years felt like an eternity. In the wake of her death, her adolescence was frozen into a brief and tragic enigma.

There is a small lake near my childhood home that sits by a sloping hill of granite rock. Behind a wall of trees, the face of the rocks display a collage of graffiti that reveals the secrets of spray-painting teenagers over the last four decades in my hometown. Among the cryptic words and arrow-pierced hearts, my sister's initials are tiny but clear in this well-known stomping ground for her and her teenage drinking friends. Though thickening trees make it harder to visit every year, I occasionally walk to this landmark and gaze at every contour of the letters for a glimpse into the soul of my sister on the night she branded that massive rock with her tiny initials. I stand in silence and try to hear the sounds and watch the sights of that anonymous night. Was she laughing while she wrote? Was she scared? Was she proud?

I have always been dissatisfied with both my knowledge of my sister's soul as well as my understanding of her teenage experience. The drive to understand Linda—to know her and accompany her on her tumultuous teenage journey—has led me to live and work in the presence of teenagers as an observer and a listener. I want to catch the hints my sister and all teenagers drop to see if anyone notices them fall. I have such curiosity for their words and ideas—a curiosity that I have always known was born in silent grief for my sister's brief life. I do not know what my sister would have said about her soul, or how she would have described it, but I see so many of her behaviors and struggles played out by teenagers in my life every day. When I hear them speak about the soul, at times I catch myself piecing together a definition that perhaps my sister would have woven. For years now I have been listening to teens speak about the soul, and the experience has convinced me that it is the key to unlocking their spiritual worlds. An adolescent's definition of the soul does not tell us everything about his or her spiritual life, yet for me it is the door into the sacred space of their spiritual imagination that holds every truth there is. I will never know how close I am to finding my sister's definition of the soul, but that uncertainty is a powerful motive to keep listening.

My mission in this book is to tell you what our teenagers are saying, right now, about their own lives, and give you the words they are using for their deepest thoughts and experiences. Often I sit in restaurants or cafes with other adults who are full of questions about my days in the hallways and classrooms of a typical high school. Most adults, no matter how distant from children or teenagers, never completely lose their curiosity for what young people are saying or doing. Conversations with my adult peers never fail to awaken memories of their high school days and cause them to blush or burst into smiles and laughter. For some, the whole process of schooling was a nightmare; for others, the memories are sweet and nostalgic; for most, growing up in school and at home was a roller coaster of emotional highs and lows. Some adults still relate and connect to the teenager they once were; others feel completely disconnected from that ancient adolescent self. But it never takes more than a few minutes of my stories for someone to interrupt me and pose the perennial adult questions: "How can you take teenagers so seriously? What do *they* know about the *real* world? They haven't even left home yet! They've never paid a bill, bought a car, got a good job, or earned a diploma. Their lives have barely begun. They don't know anything about real money or real love. They don't even know what they don't know."

Yes, it is a constant temptation to listen to the talk of teens and take them too literally or to forget the fact of their only recent and ongoing maturation. The best research on the teen's developing brain tells us that the prefrontal cortex (the center of complex thoughts, analytical power, and executive functions) does not even finish growing until one's early to mid-twenties. Parents and teachers cannot serve as mature mentors or engaged educators if they make the mistake of taking the talk of teens at face value. Finding the truths amid their tales requires patience, as well as humility in the face of their authentic human experiences. We must, if we are to earn the title "adult," exercise critical reflection on their expressions, however inspiring or insightful, in light of their developmental limitations. Making meaning with adolescent expressions is often an art and always a vocation.

Yet having said that, what about the quality of conversation among *adults* in cafes and restaurants anywhere in this country? Lean your ear toward your adult peers as they talk to each other or whisper (loudly) into their cell phones in public. Don't you hear the same kind of knee-jerk, misinformed, heated, accusatory, clueless, self-serving, and goofy statements on politics, current events, or relationships? If we are honest with ourselves, the tone and substance of many of our own conversations in the "adult" world are not that much different from those I hear in front of lockers in high school hallways. Just because our brains are capable of greater levels of thought, appreciation, creativity, virtue, and depth does not mean that the majority of adults make use of what doctors call the "high-end real estate" of the prefrontal cortex of the adult brain. Are adult conversations more reliable transcripts of truth than those of teenagers? Only on certain subjects.

I am not discrediting the knowledge and wisdom that comes with age. I spend the majority of my days talking with young people about their moral and ethical challenges and choices, and I can tell you that they need a lot of input and investment from morally mature adults if they are to survive and thrive. Young people need adults to use and share every ounce of their acquired wisdom on how to navigate a moral and spiritual life in this broken but beautiful world. Only a fool would say that an adult is no more equipped to understand themselves or their world than an adolescent. But in the area of spiritual things—of observation, experience, and reflection on the core realities of love, hope, faith, and loss in life—let us not too quickly consider the words of young people as simply naïve or childish. People of all ages have souls and therefore we all have the unfolding story of our soul to share at every age and stage of our lives with anyone willing to listen. I would be an ungrateful thief if I did not credit so many teenagers for enlarging my understanding of myself, of the world, of love, and of God. Their vision and clarity is not as strong and informed as it will be later in their lives, but I would still jump out of the way if even a small child claimed to see something falling on my head. Lack of clarity obscures truth; it does not make it impossible. Real souls have real experiences. Our souls give us all something to say and to share with everyone, as soon as we are able to start saying it.

I do encounter a small number of adults who say that they do not care what young people think about what is true or real. But it is rare to meet an adult who does not care about what young people *do,* in their homes or their neighborhoods. We are all affected in some way by the maturation process of teens and are therefore all invested in how young people are perceiving and participating in the world. The reality is that teenage perceptions, however narrow or flawed, will direct their thoughts, actions, and imagination. Whether it is to reach teens at the heights of their abilities or to rescue them from the depths of their depressions, we must learn the languages of their hearts. Teenagers are not only the future of our society, but they are also living, breathing souls in the present with the power to bless or destroy lives around them.

What ultimately matters to me is not how qualified teens are to make their statements about themselves or the world, or how qualified I am to interpret them. What matters to me is what *matters* to adolescents. If you care about the life and health of adolescents, then you know already that it is more important that young people understand that we are *listening* than it is that we understand what they are saying. Love does not qualify anyone to know the meaning of words, but love does justify anyone who tries to listen to another soul.

If the word "soul" did not exist, we would have to invent it in order to understand the spiritual lives of teenagers. They use the word with such force and trust that I have come to see it as theirs, conveying their deepest hopes, fears, and dreams for meaning and dignity. I remember distinctly the first time I asked one of my students to define the word "soul." The conversation was all too typical of "religious talks" with teenagers; she was a pro at letting adults in her life know by her sarcastic tone that she was no one's fool and that organized religion was a threat to her commitment to individuality and freedom. But I asked her anyway. According to that day's entry in my first-year-in-teaching journal, she said, "Religion? You mean hypocrisy, hate mongering, and money-grubbing? I'm not religious." I asked about the Bible; she thought it was "scary and irrelevant." I brought up God. "God?" she asked, raising her eyebrows. "Whose God? I don't believe in anyone else's God. I'm agnostic."

At some point, as we moved through this usual transcript of teenage talk that points out the unpopularity of religious terms with this generation of young people, she mentioned the word "soul." I cannot remember exactly how it entered our chat, but I do remember that her voice changed—she used it boldly and as a dear personal possession, as if the word "soul" lived and breathed beyond traditional doctrine or dogma. I could barely wait my turn to speak: "What do you mean by the soul?" My question brought her to silence and she stared at me. After a compassionate pause, she declared confidently, "The soul . . . you know, like, *your soul.*" She patted her chest with conviction aimed to persuade. It was more like she was trying to remind me of something rather than trying to teach me something new.

"Do you mean something religious?" I asked feebly. She jumped in—"No! The soul is bigger than religion!"—and then she launched into an animated and upbeat list of synonyms, metaphors, music lyrics, and personal stories about the word. To her, the soul was a voice, a guide, a compass, a magnet, and a container of hopes, fears, dreams, and secrets. "You can feel it," she insisted, "and it tells you stuff you need to know." Clearly she was speaking of a dear friend. The conversation about religion had been pat and lifeless, but this talk of the soul burst with creativity, levity, and freedom. The use of the word "soul" had moved this awkward chat about religion into the familiar neighborhood of her personal experience of her spiritual life and the spiritual life of the world. One word brought us to a place of conversation where she felt at home and in control of her ideas, or even excited about her lack of control of them and the transcendent way those ideas and images so gracefully took control of her. She was clearly not making up these ideas; rather, she struck me as a person in full obedience to their presence in her experience. She was telling me what it is like to have a soul.

Through her use of the word "soul," she was talking about all the spiritual aspects of her being and sharing many of the spiritual aspects of her life that I, as her teacher and mentor, needed and was honored to know. In a matter of minutes, I knew about some of her deepest fears, relationship wounds, moral values, high hopes for humanity, and aspirations for a divine presence in human life. In other words, I understood her "theological anthropology"—her concept of the spiritual resources and spiritual potential of the human person. Without question, knowing this about any person's worldview yields tremendous understanding of their view of life, meaning, and purpose. It had not occurred to me before this conversation that the quickest way to discern an adolescent's theological anthropology is simply to ask them to define the word "soul."

Words that she used for herself earlier in the conversation about "religion" were fairly typical labels for the self among teenagers: agnostic, skeptic, loner. But with the concept of "soul," she was obviously speaking of something not completely synonymous with herself; something whose life and breath she shared but did not completely own, and did not want to own. Her soul was not entirely a possession of hers, though she clearly felt responsible for its health and freedom. I heard her saying that, ultimately, she *belonged* to her soul. And she seemed comfortable not to control it or understand it completely, and for her life not to constrain it. It was, for her, a kind of bridge with one part firmly within her, but another end leading out of her into a spiritual universe about which she delighted to wonder. For her, the soul was something real in her that stretched beyond her and brought her life into a larger reality of time, space, and meaning.

Many developmental psychologists practice an unfortunate reductionism with regard to the language of teenagers, arguing that the concepts of "soul" and "self" are functionally interchangeable and bring no unique insights in the self-understanding of the teenager who uses them. My experience is otherwise: I believe there is a distinction to be made between the words and concepts "self" and "soul" within the mind of teenagers with whom I have worked. All you have to do is ask preteens and teens to define the two words, and you will hear the radical difference in their descriptions. For example, an eighteen-year-old male, given the opportunity to describe freely and anonymously truths about himself in a survey, wrote: "I am a jerk, I drive way too recklessly, I text too much in class." Like many teenage boys, his self-description is negative, even if honest, portraying himself as somewhat lazy, self-centered, and dispassionate. Yet, here is his definition of the soul:

> *The soul is what comes from the heart, what you love, enjoy, and makes you truly happy. Everyone has one and knows what it is. Every single person has a different view on it. Without a soul life would be terribly different because there would be no passion.*

Year after year I have heard in adolescent language the huge gap between a young person's often negative and critical view of the self and a positive and even hopeful view of the soul. I believe this space between an adolescent's view of self and soul must be understood and explored so that it can be bridged with meaningful mentoring by adults. If we can help teens stretch their understanding of the beauty of the soul to touch and transform their view of the self, we can help them bridge the divide between the shame for one's imperfections of body or mind and the hope pouring forth like a never-ending hymn from the human soul. The teenagers with whom I have spoken over the past decade are divided people: they have a remarkable confidence in the innate spiritual beauty and power of the soul in all people *in theory,* yet they cannot seem to find a personal identity or set of skills to realize their high hopes for humanity in the practice of their daily lives. They believe humans have spiritual wholeness and worth, yet they cannot seem to find or feel this wholeness and worth for themselves.

A teenager's use of the word "soul" is perhaps the most essential expression to focus on in analyzing an adolescent's emotional and spiritual health. It is an important word not because of what we as adults think it means, but because of what teenagers say it means to them. Just ask a teenager about how they would define this word. Whether religious in any way or not at all, young people I have worked with have some notion of soul meaning. When they begin their descriptions, a window opens that helps us see their deepest assumptions and questions about life, hope, and purpose.

I have discovered three things that are true about young people and their use of the word soul. First: every student has some notion of the soul. I have simply never had a student answer back, "I have never heard of the soul before." It is hard for students— for anyone—to define the soul because there is no discernable image of it and no consensus about its essence. This ambiguity has not silenced students, but instead allowed for definitions that are as varied as the people who offer them. Second: universally, positive definitions of the soul are offered, regardless of race, gender, or socioeconomic background. Third: even among students who question its existence, I have heard no condemnation of the idea. Teens discuss it as a "place" or "space" in people where there might be peace, purpose, and rest; acceptance, communion with God, or even eternal life; identity, uniqueness, and personality. Not once in a decade of teaching has any one of my students spoken in a derogatory way about the soul. While their descriptions of most other things—family, friends, music, politics, academics—seem a constant mix of those uniquely adolescent words of rebellion, personalization, or lack of interest, the soul emerges as a thing of goodness, and even beauty and promise.

Yet rarely, if ever, do students talk about the soul by using one of the most common words of their adolescent years: "mine." They speak of "*my* music," "*my* stuff," "*my* friends," "*my* ideas," or "*my* life," but they speak of "*a* soul" or "*the* soul," as if the whole idea were a rumor that they cannot substantiate or are somehow afraid to claim as their own. The business of adolescence is to reject or to possess things and ideas in a relentless pursuit of identity. Even so, the word *soul* is left unclaimed and untrained as a tool in this personal process. While teenagers see no threat in the idea of a soul, many see no real potency for working with it either. This skill set for knowing one's soul is what I believe we must teach students in our care.

This affection for "soul" is at the very least odd among teenagers who are ever quick to strike down as many of the inherited ideas of adults as possible. One would think that "soul" would be a prize target of criticism and rejection as a word that carries for grown-ups such religious overtones. Nevertheless, for young people in our day, the word is given a kind of immunity few traditional words or concepts enjoy. That is why our adult ears should perk up and discern an interesting sign of spiritual significance whenever teenagers speak positively of an idea not of their generation without hint of rejection or suspicion. Their words about the soul are incredibly hopeful and uplifting. Even so, the beauty and power of the ideas do not seem to create confidence among teenagers that the soul can be a real tool in their lives. They hope out loud in the existence of something like a soul that animates and dignifies human life, yet they show little evidence that they know the soul within themselves.

Young people locate such resources as peace, meaning, joy, and purpose in the soul; they ask the soul to hold all these assets. Using this word in conversation creates a safe space for teenagers to dream out loud and to hope for the wholeness, and perhaps even the holiness, of humanity. Because the word belongs to no one, there is no sense of trespassing on a certain traditional meaning. Young people hear the word in their favorite music and movies, and they feel inspired to express their own narratives of meaning and love with it. They feel free with the word because who can tell them that they are wrong? The word is free for use for those who are religious and not religious, those who are open to faith and those who feel burned by it, those who hate God and those who report that they speak to God every day.

How do teens express themselves in a way that we would consider religious? Their most hopeful and faithful thoughts are not found in religious frameworks or even in the rejection of religious forms of expression, as is true for members of so-called Generation X. Contrary to much commentary on the current state of adolescents, I do not see young people expressing or finding confidence in meaning and purpose in drugs or sex—both of which get mixed reviews with young people, even among those who engage in both frequently. Nor do they put their faith in money and power—both of which are feared as much as revered among young people. However, a safe haven that their imaginations construct as a reliable resource of sacredness and purpose seems to be this thing called the "soul." At times, words about the soul are the only uncritical and wholesome things I have heard them say about humanity.

The soul is like the black box of an airplane, at times buried beneath daily consciousness by life's trivialities or tragedies, though still sending that faint signal to those who are listening and trying to get closer to the living sound. Our culture, and so often the culture of our schools, has so sadly separated young people from this inner voice—a voice implanted to lead them to peace and hope and faith. Miraculously, they still believe the soul is within every person, somewhere. If we neglect them in this search-and-rescue mission for the God-given resources of the soul, we should not be surprised to see them searching for truth, meaning, and love in every shallow hole of our culture. Adolescents cannot help searching because they hear *something*. Adolescents cannot help following because they feel drawn to follow *something*. Those of us who know the meaning and beauty in that voice of the soul need to help teenagers understand it and experience the wholeness that comes with living in the logic of their being.

The good news is that the soul of any person is not actually lost; it is deep within every person, where it was created to be. What is often lost is the adolescent's confidence that the resources they describe as being of the soul are actually within the reach of their skills to find and follow. Mentors of teenagers do not have to create souls. Through intentional love and radical hospitality becoming a habit in the living room or the classroom, teenagers will see that there is something in them worthy of our loving and honoring. Teens will respond to the passion that adults demonstrate for their spiritual selves. Teenagers will seek to understand what it is of worth that we see and celebrate in them. Young people begin to develop the skills of spirituality when they become curious enough to check out the adult-planted affirming messages about their spiritual identity. The moment a young person looks in the mirror to see what the adult who loves and names his or her soul has pointed to: this is a moment of spiritual homecoming. This is the moment when the teenager begins to feel that his or her life might indeed be sacred and priceless, not for what it does, but because that is how it was created to be.

Every teenager I have ever met is battling something. Some are battling an addiction to drugs or alcohol, while others battle minute-to-minute fears or anxieties. Most are battling the endless waves of loneliness that do not leave them even when surrounded by friends or family. A few are battling questions of sexual orientation, race, or social class in school or in their neighborhoods; still others are trying not to break down and weep on any given day because of broken home lives, unrealistic parental expectations, or fears of failure and rejection. I asked one eighteen-year-old boy a few years ago how often he felt like crying. The very gregarious athlete and captain of his team smiled at me. "You serious? You mean like, actual tears-crying?" So as not to crowd him I remained standing right next to him but kept looking straight ahead onto the field. "Yeah," I clarified, "like tears-crying." He lived with a mother who worked late hours and had dated constantly but unsuccessfully through his childhood. His father was distant in every conceivable way. Out of the corner of my eye, I could see him squint into the distance far beyond the field we were both pretending to watch. "I don't really think about crying. Like, what's the point of it? I don't want to think about it, you know? I think if I started to cry I would never stop. Who needs that drama?"

All teenagers are both blessed and bruised by their families. I have never met a teenager who felt completely understood or accepted for the collage of conflicting truths that they are. This does not mean that any or every adult in his or her life is failing: it is more a reflection of the imperfect love we offer one another, and the broken ability we all have to see, accept, and be transformed by the love of others. Teenagers are not broken solely because we have loved them in broken ways; teenagers are broken because they are human and because those of us who have raised and loved them are ourselves broken and frail in our ability to offer unconditional love. Teens are as much a product *like us* as *of us.*

So the brokenness of teens is not merely the fault of adults, but rather a fertile shared reality upon which we can build authentic connections in conversation and relationship. As the author M. Scott Peck said best in the first sentence of his classic work *The Road Less Traveled,* "Life is difficult." We are all battling something. Unconditional love cannot be a final destination for any honest but imperfect heart; it is rather the aspiration of every moment. I have never met a teenager who felt perfectly loved by adults and teachers, but I *have* met kids who describe their parents and teachers as "trying," "caring," "open to changing their minds," and "ready to apologize when they screw up." Successful loving, in the eyes of teens, comes from reaching out to know them with whatever frail or needy soul a parent or adult has.

Negative or broken views of self undermine so much of the decision-making and meaning-making of young people, but a teenager's own conceptions of the soul can challenge and even restore that self. Spiritual healing is necessary because the materialism of first-world adult America is strangling the self-confidence and self-worth of teenagers. This suffocation of spirit expresses its damage in all the high-risk behaviors too common among young people. If you listen to teenagers share their experiences of being in high-expectation families, in high-achieving schools, in competitive sports, in the college process—whether in poor families or in affluent but wounded families—you will come away convinced that the world we have presented to young people is often scaring and shaming our teenagers. We tolerate a culture that daily questions the beauty of each child's soul by constantly holding our young people up to judgment. The challenge for adults is to learn and then to teach young people the skills of listening to, believing in, and living out of the truths of their conception of the soul; to invite adolescents to embody their own spiritual ideas in their daily decisions and actions. Our actions—not just our words—need to show teenagers that we agree with their hope in the existence of the soul and that we are ready to live in light of the dignity of the souls in all people.

Adolescents need us to tell them they are right about the soul. A bright young female high school student I met in Tacoma, Washington, shared her definition of the soul as a "soloist in my heart singing to me and keeping me sane." When I asked her if this idea came from a religious upbringing or from her parents, she gave me a blank stare. "My parents?" She looked down at her pink shoes and searched for an answer among the worn knots of her rainbow shoelaces as if she had never thought about the question. "I don't know what my parents think about the soul. I don't think they believe in stuff like that."

Being raised in a culture calling them to live both in *and* of the world has caused many of our teenagers to lose their way— prodigal children who have gone too far in their thinking and feeling from the homing beacon of their soul to return on their own. The chasm between their dark statements of doubt about themselves and their hopeful statements about their souls is the proof of this crisis of homecoming. If adolescents are to find their way back to a knowledge and confidence of belonging to and being loved unconditionally by God and authentically by others, we have to help them build a bridge from critical self-doubt to a solid spiritual identity and confidence. I call this "soul-esteem," and it is the ability to define one's self not just according to the words of others or the values of the world, but also by the feelings and resources that spring naturally and continually from the soul.

In reaching out to build such bridges in the self-concept of young people, adults must learn to use teen language. Adolescent definitions of the soul show that they have cognitive understanding of the spiritual identity and wholeness available to all human beings, but this knowledge of the soul is not at work in their lives to inform or enliven their view of self. We adults have to understand the gaps between self-criticism and soul beauty, one teenager at a time, and then help them to apply their confidence in the creativity and goodness of the soul to their views of self.

Whenever I ask a student to define the soul, I also ask how they define themselves: "If, as you say, the soul is wise, caring, and comforting, are you?" Blank stares. Most teenagers, and even pre-teens, are intelligent enough to understand the logic that if the soul is beautiful and, according to their beliefs, all people have souls, then all people share this beauty. But experience shows me that this last step—moving from convictions or dreams about the soul toward a confidence that the soul's attributes are part of the adolescent person—is a skill most of them do not have.

Rather than write a script in our own language to help kids connect with their innate spiritual convictions, a better method for adults is to give teenagers their best words back to them, along with our unconditional love and affirmation. Their heads already hold the liberating truths, so mentoring teenagers who are moving from self-doubt to soul-esteem is not a matter of teaching them new truths. It is a matter of affirming their developing sense of who they are, that the human soul is real, and that their hopes in the guidance and goodness of the soul are the beginning of wisdom, wholeness, and peace. It is not that students do not believe in their own ideas: just look at their music collections, tattoos, or T-shirts. Teens write about their ideas, tattoo them on their bodies, download music about them, pierce their skin with metal or plastic signs of them, and employ the word "soul" as their most powerful word when they describe the highs and lows of their intimate relationships. But these ideas lie dormant because, as we will discuss in the next chapter, the prevailing definitions of success in this society are about what we do and not what we are. As one wise boy once said to me in frustration, "People define you by what you've done at the end of the day, not by what you are before the day starts. I know I could accomplish more in a day if I thought I didn't have to prove anything."

We adults are equally confused about the soul, and young people often mirror our uncertainty. Many churches and synagogues

I have visited across the country speak only rarely about the soul's actual role in human life, despite the fact that their scriptures and hymns rely on and rhapsodize about the soul constantly. When people of faith do preach or write in their bulletins about the soul, few actual definitions or illustrations are offered as to what the soul has to do with daily life. It seems fairly clear that the soul comes from God and will return to the creator after death, but there is not much said about the *role* of the soul between the womb and the tomb. We cannot expect young people to develop skills with something we have neglected to tell them is a tool.

An adolescent's fragile but no less creative and dynamic language for spiritual life has little or no connection with much of the language found in the scriptures of the mainline religions. Many students have positive associations with "spirituality" or "faith," while "organized religion" is most often viewed with skepticism, if not anger or total rejection. When my students defend their rejection of religion, many do so by describing their experiences of church or synagogue in a way that makes religious thought and practice unpalatable for thoughtful people of any age. And many describe the alienation they feel in many churches, synagogues, and mosques when they encounter overt or covert demands for what they perceive to be self-denying uniformity amid unexplained and eccentric rituals in ancient language. But despite this frustration, I have yet to meet a student who rejects spirituality as a capacity or habit for people of any age. There is simply no discernable anger among teenagers over the spiritual promise or practice of lives, whether or not the student engages in either. They possess hope, and even pride, in their spiritual potential and the spiritual potential of the world.

However, communicating with young people about their spiritual life in a way that disarms their defenses against conventional religion means speaking in their terms, not ours. We must respect their curiosity and even passion for spiritual realities. I believe that traditional religious communities actually share many truths found in adolescent talk of spirituality; we have more in common than either generation might think. But we need to find out which spiritual words and concepts have currency with young people in order to translate the timeless truths of our traditions into timely teenage speech. In their definitions of the soul I have found a whole world of ideas that any parent, teacher, or spiritual mentor would want to pursue with young people. Knowing how adolescents define the spiritual life—specifically, how they think their own soul works in making the spiritual life possible—is essential for adults who want to understand what teenagers do and can believe.

Knowing the soul exists is a work of the mind; feeling, hearing, and loving the soul is a practice of the imagination. But the performance-based culture we have created for our kids is causing an atrophy of their imagination and is disabling their ability to *feel* what they already *think* about the soul. They experience degrees of self-doubt and self-criticism as a matter of daily experience in our winner-takes-all world. These judgments rob them of the spiritual peace necessary to hear the soul within them or to make healthy decisions in all areas of life based on the direction the human soul can give.

Theologians speak of "theological anthropology" as the collection of ideas individuals hold about the possibilities of divine presence in human beings along with their potential for a full spiritual life. It is essential that we understand an adolescent's theological anthropology and use it as our linguistic road map, for when we know the theological presuppositions of teenagers we know three things about them. First, we learn what *identity* young people believe they possess to ground an emotional, intellectual, and spiritual life. In other words, we learn *who* they think they are, and perhaps for the more theologically inclined teenagers, we learn *whose* they think they are. Second, we learn what *purpose* they believe their life and gifts might serve in the world. And third, we learn what *capacity* they see in themselves for moral and spiritual vocation and courage. We cannot, as parents and teachers, appeal to the theological imagination and heroism of the teenager until we know and appreciate their understood capacity for a spiritual life. We may want to change their understanding of these three pieces of their self-concept; we may want to add, subtract, stretch, or transform their view of spiritual life. But we need to know both their starting points and the horizon of their hopes.

Listen to this definition of the soul written by a twelfth-grade girl:

> *A soul is your true self—all that you are, all that you keep hidden, all that you show the world. It is your thoughts, feelings, emotions—everything that you ever were or could be. It's your good side, your demons, your gray areas. You don't have to show the world what your soul is, but it's there. It's everything that is not physical in you. It's your heart and mind together, and it creates your true self. The soul is there to give you individuality, to guide your morals, emotions, humanity. It is you defined. Often it can be your best friend, sometimes your worst enemy. It's all of your voices combined into a single, multifaceted intangible yet very real thing, unique to each of us. For me it's internal dialogue—by thinking so much about myself, my beliefs, my morals, I can more clearly see my soul and understand it. My soul matters so much to me—it's what guides me, wrongly or rightly, it's everything I am, good and bad. It's what makes me me. I couldn't live without it. It brings me to new realizations, new ideas, new reasons to be happy. Without it, I'd be a shell. Literally. I would have nothing worthwhile to offer to the world.*

In this young woman's definition, we see all three essential parts of an adolescent's theological anthropology that we need to know in order to guide her into spiritual skills and practices. We read about the *identity* the soul brings her: "It's what makes me *me*." We read about the moral content of the soul giving direction and *purpose* to her life: "Without it, I'd be a shell. Literally. I would have nothing worthwhile to offer to the world." And third, this soul definition clearly shows her confidence in the spiritual capacity of the soul: "It brings me to new realizations, new ideas, new reasons to be happy." But it is also worth noting that this definition comes from a young woman who describes herself in deeply negative terms that seem to contradict the beauty and power of the soul:

I expect to succeed without working too hard, which is bad.
I am a really good liar because people don't really expect it
of me.
I don't work hard but I still do well, so I'm worried about
what will happen when I'm faced with something that
requires me to try. I'm not sure I have the work ethic to
get it done.

Clearly, this same student who credits the soul with giving her "new ideas" and "new realizations" cannot draw from her own soul the power to live a more honest life, as well as the energy to form a strong work ethic. Her admission of frequent lying explains the disharmony that leads her to refer to the moral voice of the soul as both "best friend" and "worst enemy." Sadly, the soul that rescues her from being a mere "shell" is not, in her own words, aiding her in the construction of an honest work ethic for a successful life.

In this one student's definition, we see the reality that will be the focus of this book. When asked to list "truths about herself," this young woman's self-doubt and self-criticism are untouched by her high estimation of the worth, power, and beauty of her soul. In short, she thinks more highly of her soul than of herself. Student after student in this book will demonstrate a similar contradiction between the weaknesses of the self and the strengths of the soul. Returning to this young woman who says the soul is her best friend, we read her brave honesty about moral failures ("gray areas"), paired with equally bold definitions and defenses of her soul.

For me it's internal dialogue—by thinking so much about
myself, my beliefs, my morals, I can more clearly see my soul
and understand it. My soul matters so much to me—it's what
guides me.

Her awareness of the soul is the fruit of self-analysis. Again, it is interesting that analysis of her self results in self-criticism, whereas analysis of the soul's role in her life gives rise to love and admiration. She says her soul "guides" her, but by her own admission that she is a liar, we realize that it does not. Thus she hears the soul, but is unable to follow it. The work of any potential mentor to her should begin with noticing this contradiction between self and soul, and then helping the student in building bridges between the two. For although she can see the moral and spiritual clarity that her soul provides, she lacks a set of skills to steer the ship of her thoughts and actions according to that spiritual tracker beam.

I ask students to define the word "soul" because of all the terms associated with faith or spirituality, it is the one with which they are the most comfortable. It never fails to open a window into their deepest spiritual ideas and experiences. The word is so ubiquitous in our culture—used to describe anything from food and music to perfume and cars—that kids feel free to employ it themselves. Teenagers have an infinite number of definitions for this word, but these beautifully varied definitions point in most cases to something meaningful that enhances life, establishes human dignity, and transcends the physical world. Trained theologians and philosophers might find the adolescent uses of this word clumsy, contradictory, and ambiguous, but many of these same intellectuals use similar adjectives for adolescence itself. But if those of us who are parents, teachers, and mentors can see adolescent statements of spiritual truth as authentically stating needs rather than irreverently rewriting creeds, we can perhaps start an intimate conversation rather than conduct a distancing diagnosis of the young people in our lives. Too many teens are convinced that those of us in the adult community do not know the difference between diagnosis and dialogue. Educators understand the need for both, but it is my students who have never failed to show me how little commitment I sometimes show to the practical work of honest dialogue.

It is teenagers who have also helped me to understand what authentic talk of spirituality means and sounds like, and what fruits of understanding it can bear. To ask adolescents for a definition of the soul is very often to strike gold. Not everyone pours forth in words; most struggle for a few sentences until they find words that are true and meaningful, while some seem unable to find words at all. But those who do have taught me much about their spiritual lives and about what might lay behind the silence of their less loquacious peers.

In the following chapters we will hear much more of what adolescents have to say about the world around them, about their parents and friends, about their fears for the future. What are the stakes of ignoring the immature, confusing, and beautiful words of teenagers about their souls and their experiences? On the one hand, there is the possibility that the ideas and visions of teenagers can in fact enhance and expand our own understanding of what it means to be human. On the other hand, there is the price of abandoning the voice of the adolescent. And what might that price be? Ask Shakespeare. The closing scene of *Romeo and Juliet* is the opening statement for taking teenagers as seriously as we can.

 *Chapter Two*

NAP TIME IS OVER

Teenagers Looking at the World

"I know I don't want to grow up to be like either of my parents, but one of my greatest fears is losing them."

L *ord of the Flies* is read by millions of middle school and high school students in this country every year. This haunting novel by Nobel Prize-winning author William Golding chronicles a group of British schoolboys marooned on a deserted island who try to survive and create a community without the aid of adults. Now separated from the adult authors and enforcers of civilization, the once well-mannered schoolboys soon abandon their domestication, discover the darker depths of human nature, and turn on each other in acts of cruel tribalism, bullying, violence, and even murder of their own peers. *TIME* magazine chose Golding's allegorical testimony of the brutality possible in human nature as one of the one hundred best English-language novels of the twentieth century. This 1954 novel has been selected for reading and reflection by thousands of English teachers across America for over fifty years. Reading this work and writing some kind of "what it all means" essay is a rite of passage for preteens and teens in our educational system.

Why is this novel so popular in English classrooms? Ask any teacher (I have asked many), and he or she will tell you that students enjoy its resonance with the stressful social structures of adolescent life. One of my students once called it "the best nonfiction documentary of middle school life ever!" Students recognize the island in *Lord of the Flies* as their own isolated state, where the happy hopes of childhood become cold and frightened under the dark shadow of approaching adolescent life. Similar to Golding's lush island, middle and high school hallways teem with strange colors, sounds, smells, and surges of growth that introduce boundless beauty alongside fearful inequality. The physical differences of skin color, size, and ability once celebrated in elementary school surface in adolescence as potential liabilities and even commodities at the onset of puberty. As one fourteen-year-old female student once wrote on a survey, "I didn't realize how lucky I was to be tall in elementary school, but now I know IT MATTERS." By high school it becomes clear that these differences are not passing, but are instead permanent realities impervious to the forces of change that were trained, trusted, and prized in childhood, such as creativity, hard work, or hope. You are shorter than other people and that will not change. You are learning disabled and that will not change. You are awkward at sports and that will not change. Your skin color makes you stand out and that will not change. One ninth-grade boy lamented in a survey:

> *I don't ever remember feeling limited in grade school. You could join everything then. But now ... no deal. Everywhere I turn, I get shut out, not picked, not cast, and not even called to hang out! I had no idea how few things I'm ok enough to do.*

Older high school students who have taken their share of classes in the biological sciences love to state this similar frustration in fewer words. As a senior boy said to me last year while we were working on his college admission essays, "Is it me or is life ALL ABOUT natural selection?"

Elementary school, at its best, celebrates human differences and finds a role if not an award for every kind of person. But take a walk down any middle school hallway in America and you will see the adroit instincts of self-defense in human nature exploding early in the second decade of life. Middle school students practice clumsy but clear conformity in an effort to create safe spaces in their relational lives; they blunt their blossoming differences in height, weight, skin color, desires, and personality by dressing, talking, buying, and lying along with everyone else. And who can blame them? Anyone who mocks the safety that preteens and teens seek in conforming to the crowd knows little of the pandemic of bullying in every school in this country. If you do not understand why teens conform, then you do not understand what teens face.

That is why I am not surprised by how often young people I meet in schools across the country refer directly to *Lord of the Flies* as they describe their own moral challenges. Girls and boys testify to the reality of meanness that not only visits but also plagues adolescent social life, among all races and social classes. I have heard the phrase "It's like *Lord of the Flies*" so often over the past decade that I decided to keep notes of when and where students used it. So far, I have heard it from both girls and boys in rural Pennsylvania, New York City, an affluent parochial school in Boston, a failing public school in Detroit, an all-honors academy in Seattle, a magnet school in Dayton, a one-room schoolhouse in West Virginia, and a charter school in Chicago. I even remember a friend who wrote his college admission essay on Golding's novel and why it explained his parents' choice to homeschool their children. This disturbing tale of the potential beast lurking in the human soul is a touchstone for American youth because it offers creative arguments for the potential for evil in each of us, knit into an accessible tale about children on an island. For adolescents it furnishes an explanation for the pain, sadness, and fear so many of them experience by portraying human nature as the source of brokenness, as something to be feared once the parental police of any culture disappear. Golding's message, as I have heard it told and retold among young people, is that the philosopher Thomas Hobbes was right about human beings when he wrote in his *Leviathan* over four hundred years ago, *Homo homini lupus est*—"Every man is a wolf to other men."

Games played and songs sung in elementary school catechize the notion that every person is a friend and neighbor, but every adolescent is learning just the opposite. As their elementary school teachers and Little League coaches slowly recede further away from the social world of preteens and teens, it becomes clear that the fairness doctrines of childhood recede along with grown-ups, hinting that such rules of the road were in fact adult impositions rather than natural laws. You may think the middle schoolers and high schoolers in your life want to be forever free from grown-up presence. They may breathe fire in your face for hanging around the new social scenes of their adolescent island, but I know for a fact that a deep part of them also breathes easier when some adult lifeguard is on duty.

There is another phenomenally popular novel about human nature, also published in 1954 and recently made into a major motion picture. Few teenagers today have not seen the movie version of *The Lord of the Rings* and its sequels. Educators and commentators complain often about the shrinking attention span of this generation of young people, but it is amazing how many teens have read the thick tomes by J. R. R. Tolkien that inspired this epic film empire. The books and the films have become a mammoth global media success, grossing over a billion dollars worldwide.

The subtitle of the first of these blockbuster films is significant: *The Fellowship of the Ring*. "Fellowship" marks the profoundly different and far more positive message of Tolkien's worldview than the Darwinian darkness of the island in *Lord of the Flies*. All three Tolkien films known so well to contemporary teens celebrate the enduring friendships of characters that each play their unique parts in saving the world from evil. Each character has a sense of individual mission, as well as a strong sense of shared responsibility for the well-being and safety of others. Individualism and selfish desire are the epicenters of evil; committed friends and their covenant communities are the hope of the world. When one friend falls into danger, despair, or deceit, it is peers who rescue, restore, and reanimate. This notion that fellowship and friendship are the means to heal the world is also the focal point of J. K. Rowling's *Harry Potter* books. Like Tolkien before her but without the strong undertow of his cryptic theological themes, Rowling presents fellowship as the secret weapon against evil, and friendship as the true heroism.

Tolkien has a keen sense of evil as a force actively destroying beauty and devouring holiness. He portrays its darkness with complexity and imagery that dwarfs any prose in Golding's *Lord of the Flies.* Tolkien rejects Golding's thesis that human nature is the real beast on the island that can only be tamed when the law-enforcers of culture return and rescue. Tolkien argues instead that human nature is both a threat to but also the hope of salvation. For this ardent Roman Catholic, there is both hedonism *and* heroism knit into human nature. But in the transformative power of relationships with others and with the divine, each person can be enlightened to his or her own incredible and innate moral direction and courage. Tolkien's message, as I have heard it repeated and admired by teens, is that we can fall into degradation, but we can also dig ourselves out of it with the aid of loyal friends. As one boy wrote to me in a cartoon he drew about not making the football team that year, "I am short, but so are Hobbits, and they saved the world."

For Golding's characters it is the opposite: the membrane in human nature between man and beast is so thin that it can be shed and shred as easily as a schoolboy's uniform on a hot beach. Society is so fragile that all it took for friends to degrade into enemies was the weakening of social customs that turned out to be as parochial and impermanent as school clothes. But in the great global battle of good and evil on Tolkien's Middle Earth, friends and their fellowship are the timeless and triumphant *axis mundi* for the hope and salvation of all creation.

Over the past ten years I have gathered two lists of descriptions of the world—one offered by girls and one by boys, based on my collected responses from twelfth graders to this question: *"Tell me things that are true about the world."* I first ask teenagers to write out their own truths about the world as they see it. I then hand out accumulated lists of popular answers from prior years, representing the voices of different social classes, races, and geographic regions. The restaurant booths, classrooms, and meeting rooms across the country in which I have handed out these lists often remain silent for many minutes. Students have a natural respect for the words and points of view of other teenagers. They may not agree, but high school is such an unyielding experience of reading the thoughts of adults that students always show initial respect and even awe for anything in their hands that came from the mouths of other young people. Of course, criticisms and corrections eventually flow, but I am always struck by the initial silence of students when an adult hands them printed material written by teenagers.

What you will hear in these responses to my question about what is true about the world is that students see a *Lord of the Flies* world of cruelty and natural selection haunted by a *Lord of the Rings* hope for friendship and fellowship. As witness to the world that adults have created and accepted, these teen statements represent what they have heard and learned from both adult talking and adult nonverbal modeling. When you listen to the talk of teens about the world they see and hear, and you want to know where these ideas come from, you have to take a trip back to the day they were born. It is a long trip of listening to every word spoken or left unspoken in the family car, at the dinner table, on the youth athletic field, on the stage, on the family trip, in the pews, in the moments of crisis: these words and the events that framed them all matter, and they all sculpt the soul of the adolescent.

I have focused most of my research on students I have met or taught in their last year of high school. In their twelfth-grade year, many students have already begun to encounter and experience the rhythms and realities of the adult world as they stand on the boundary of the sheltered bubbles of home and high school life. Many already have paying jobs, many have begun to travel, and others have begun to develop their own consumption habits. Certainly the college process for those who enter it introduces high school students to the mysterious metrics that rule our country's meritocracies of academics, athletics, and other performance subcultures for young people.

I have heard it said often, and usually with humor, that adults should avoid asking high school seniors about their views of reality precisely because of the level of anxiety, uncertainty, and frustration brought on by leaving high school or entering the college process. Many students do have an overly negative perception of or anger about the patterns of the world because of stress over college admissions or simply the exhaustion of high school. But rather than discount or write-off the critical words of unhappy teens, I want to know *why* there is so much frustration and angst. They may in fact be "overreacting," but what are they overreacting *to*? I do not believe stress, at any age, is completely a figment of the imagination, nor is criticism or complaining somehow innate in teenagers. There are reasons behind their negativity, as listening to teenagers will soon reveal.

———————

Verbatim responses written by twelfth-grade girls
in answer to this question:
"Tell me things that are true about the world."

You can never be certain about anything.
Cheating does get you ahead professionally.
Doing the right thing is often unrewarding.
You are the only person you can trust, truly.
When you don't have established guidelines to live by, you
*   will be swept away.*
Only bad things are in the news.
People aren't usually willing to help other people unless it
*   involves very little effort.*
There's more hate than love.
The world is cruel to the underdogs.
People assume that possessions bring happiness.
The world needs guidance and strength from good people.
Peace is not possible.
The world needs more love.
People like war.
Everything is competition.
The world is extremely materialistic.
Honesty can sometimes screw you over, even if it's the right
*   thing to do.*
Secrets don't stay secrets for very long.
The ends justify the means, period.
Nice guys finish last unless they know the right people.

Lying has just become an acceptable form of living.
There is an impossible amount of information to know
about the world.
To get ahead, it's all about who you know.
We are wasteful and many people realize it and do nothing.
We are obsessed with competition and success.
We are uncomfortable with the people we really are.
We've forgotten how to love and I think that's the saddest
part of this world.
It really does matter how much money you have.
So many people just pretend that they care about important
things.
The world is not very forgiving.
The world is too fast-paced (people need to slow down and
enjoy life).
You only have one life and you never know when it could be
taken away.
The world is too competitive.
It's a harsh world out there.
Survival of the fittest.
Peace is only an ideal.
There will always be someone who is better than you at
something.
People are untrustworthy, but despite that, people do need
other people.
The world is never going to be fair.

Verbatim responses written by twelfth-grade boys
in answer to this question:
"Tell me things that are true about the world."

Nap time is over.
Nice guys finish last. Always.
The world is not as accepting as I once thought.
Not everyone is here to help.

*People cheat, people lie, people steal and there's nothing you
    can do about it.*

*The world can be so hurtful that you wish you could
    disappear; it can be so wonderful you are speechless.*

*The world is a far scarier place than we know or have been
    taught.*

*The world is afraid of difference in appearance, race, and
    social economic status.*

Most people have trouble practicing what they preach.

*The best way to deal with complex and serious issues is
    through satire, by laughing at yourself.*

The world has become an angry place.

Culture doesn't have its priorities straight.

The future is looking bleaker than the present.

*People often isolate themselves from the real world because
    it's easier.*

*Humanity is currently in a bad place as far as getting along
    with each other.*

It is hard to find peace.

Money can get you out of any situation.

To be successful, someone else has to fail.

People don't actually care about other people's well-being.

*People can't be trusted and will always look out for
    themselves first.*

Most things are not how they appear.

No one cares unless you win.

*Unless what you are saying has something to do with them,
    people won't listen.*

Girls are crazy.

I hate the world, but I used to love it.

It pays to cheat.

Love should be number one, but it isn't.

Honest people cannot survive.

Being nice and helpful lets others step all over you.

Everyone has enemies.

*You can cheat your way through life (no matter how sad
    and pathetic that is).*

Survival of the fittest.

It is hard to be the good guy.
Fair is dead.
If you don't have connections you can't survive.
Life is a game, it's all about who plays to win.
The world is so much different than what I was led to think.
People can be terrible to each other.
You have to lie and cheat to get to the top.
The winners write history.
Men are animals that have been given the chance to be
*   something more, but we rarely take it.*
Peace is a lie because somewhere in the world at any given
*   moment they're throwing children into mass graves.*
*   That's the way it's always been and the way it will*
*   always be.*

Welcome to life on Golding's island, where you are only as valuable as you are popular, you are only worth what you win, and above all, you must always watch your back. These samples represent only a fraction of my research on student perceptions of the world, but the trends do not change much from school to school, city to city, or year to year. What is clear is that teens feel hounded by extremely high expectations and haunted by the cruelty of endless competitiveness. Being seen as successful is a cutthroat game that one needs to learn and play sooner rather than later. You have to find a "marketable skill" early on and then master it before anyone else does—or at least keep up with everyone else's race toward mastery. And the result of all this competition ("Nobody cares unless you win") is, unfortunately, not an increase in self-confidence. As one young woman stated wisely, "We are uncomfortable with the people we really are." The world our teens perceive looks a lot like Golding's fictional island, where being famous is more powerful than being faithful. Money is more powerful than relationships. Fear is more normal than joy. The world is more confusing than inspiring. People are more self-interested than helpful. The ends justify the means. Being moral is hard. Being spiritual is harder. And peace, by any definition, is ultimately not possible. According to teenagers, there are rules in our world, but these rules are not more powerful than money, and in any setting, rules are rarely fair. As one boy states, "Fair is dead." If you are going to follow a moral code, it must be your own because the adult world appears to lack any universal ethic. In the words of one female: "When you don't have established guidelines to live by, you will be swept away."

There is also a palpable sense of sadness and mourning that the real world can be so mean, so unsafe, and so unlike the world they were told about as children. As one boy puts it, "I hate the world, but I used to love it," and a young girl echoes his sadness: "The world is so much different than I was led to think." One male student of mine wrote in a college essay about the hard transition from being a child to being an adolescent:

> It was always my goal in elementary school to be the Nice Guy. I also felt it was my parents' and teachers' goal for me too. But I learned during high school that being the nice guy means being called gay, being seen as weak and usually coming in last.

This generation of young people has been in more clubs, in more scout troops, and on more teams than any other in the history of the country, so you can understand why they are so upset at the lack of team spirit they see in the world around them. They observe:

> There's more hate than love.
> Not everyone is here to help.
> The world is cruel to the underdogs.
> The world has become an angry place.

A generation that was told and tutored in the importance of practice and performing has come to a sad realization that "no one cares unless you win."

In elementary school, many of these young people were taught to notice and celebrate the differences among people. And yet adolescence brings on a sense that "the world is afraid of difference in appearance, race, and economic status." The core tenet of any religion is to love one's neighbor, and yet our teens observe:

"Love should be number one, but it isn't." Many teens believe that the world waiting for them only rewards winners and teases or ignores the Nice Guy. But these adolescent expressions are not just grumbling: there is also *grief* in the words of my students about the state of the world, and this grief actually gives me hope. Grief is more than complaint. Grief is also a form of emotional or spiritual protest, whose energy flows from the collision of hope and hurt. Adolescent words about the unkindness of the world and their sadness in response say to me that teens have not given up completely on themselves as change agents in the world or in their dreams for meaningful relationships defined by fairness and friendship. Their pain persists because their hope persists. Teens protest the shallowness of popular norms of behavior because they still believe in the depth of dignity within all human beings. The conviction in every chapter of *Lord of the Rings* that fellowship ennobles individuals and that friendship saves the world touches and affirms the hopes of teenagers that life *does* have fixed but liberating moral rules, that humanity is at least as beautiful as it is frightening, and that working together is not only more enjoyable but also more productive than merely competing with and defeating others.

So despite the *Lord of the Flies* world our adolescents witness on their televisions, in their schools, and at times in their own homes, there is still a tenuous belief among adolescents in the possible triumph of fellowship over competition. A senior boy laments, "I need my friends, but the same colleges can't take all of us, so I feel like we're already pulling away from one another." Teens feel the pressure to see their peers as wolves rather than friends. And it pains them to make choices with time and energy that avoid hurting adult expectations and yet also reject their innate longing for true connection with others. A twelfth-grade boy sums up the split-screen world that troubles his soul: "The world can be so hurtful that you wish you could disappear; it can be so wonderful you are speechless." Teens prize friendship, but they feel the pull of parental pressure, school-based meritocracies, or other high expectations toward material success. We carve out little time for teens to practice friendship.

They also sense that success has a price, because it pulls them away from investing time and energy in meaningful relationships and in the more private project of building moral courage and vision. It is amazing to me that as a society we hold such high expectations for marriage when, in fact, our adolescents receive so little encouragement and training in relationship-building or promise-making during the first two decades of life. Ask teenagers to tell you whether or not they are rewarded or even directed toward investments in friendship and they will bear witness to the marginalization of friendships in favor of the meritocracies of the material world. We reward teens for acts of individualism, competitive prowess, and external achievements while we know as adults that marriage and other commitments in adult life require instead the practice of partnership, sensitivity, joy for private victories, and delayed gratification. The loyalties of the heart of teens are often torn between pleasing adults or pursuing friendships or other more spiritual patterns in life that consume time and threaten individualistic or socially rewarded outcomes. One female said it best:

> *I hope I make real friends in college. That's my biggest hope for college. I hope I have a best friend who is a real best friend, not like the ones I have now who are just the people who I do the most things with. I wish I had best friends now. I need a best friend now. But there's no time. My parents want me to be a good friend, but not at the expense of anything else they want me to do. I only have time to get to know the people who are trying to do the same things as me.*

While the hit television talent show "American Idol" bespeaks the current national obsession for watching individuals compete frantically for the thumbs-up from a national mob of millions of viewers, a different reality television show called "The Amazing Race" has been around for just as many years, with its own throngs of millions of viewers tuning in weekly to watch *teams* instead of individuals compete in international scavenger hunts. Both television shows have won awards for pulling in viewers every year, but the diametrically opposed messages of these two elimination-as-entertainment reality shows serve as yet another example of the bipolar messages we send and celebrate with our young people—messages that pit friendship against winning. What is remarkable about "The Amazing Race" is that the teams are not made up of celebrities or television personalities. Rather, teams consist of pairs of brothers, sisters, parents and children, spouses, or close friends. They are all racing to win, but the only way to win this game is to work as a team better than everyone else is working to be a team.

The vastly different narratives of these two popular reality shows point again to the divided longings of the broader culture that teenagers merely adopt and reflect. "The Amazing Race" is a hymn to the power of fellowship. Every pair that fails in every season of this show fails for the same reason: they did not work together. Individualism is the only but ever-present enemy. The increasing popularity of fellowship as the truest freedom and the most fulfilling success in films and television hints that the cultural tides of this new century are perhaps pulling away from the island of *Lord of the Flies,* albeit slowly. Shows like "The Amazing Race" that depict the power of committed relationships and teamwork or suggest that the individualistic winner/loser plotline so popular among Baby Boomer and Generation X media-producers and consumers might finally be giving way to messages more resonant with the longings of the soul of the adolescent.

The decades of ever-increasing materialism that emerged in the euphoric wake of winning the Second World War have collapsed into a global recession so public and so pervasive in our country that no young person can avoid seeing the accident scene and the moral lessons rising in the smoke. We are at a rare and priceless moment with adolescents. We have the opportunity to reach out to teens with lessons our own materialism have taught us and affirm the timeless longings of the teenage soul. Adolescents want to believe what we told them in primary school, despite the fact that many of us grow silent or abandon the script for meaning and purpose when fears for our children's future set in. Teens believe that individual gifts and lives find their place and joy not on a podium standing alone, but rather in fellowships that transform strangers into neighbors and competitors into friends.

Despite all the talk of how much time teens spend playing video games or competitive sports, the average teenager in America today spends the most amount of his or her free time on the Internet social networking site called Facebook, where there are no uniforms, no scoreboards, and no winners or losers. In short, Facebook is not a sport or a game *per se*. It is simply a place in space to connect with other people. This is a new cultural phenomenon and it is a hopeful change as far as trends among adolescents are concerned. One Baby Boomer parent bore witness to these hopeful winds of cultural change with this comment she shared in an email.

> *I don't get why so many people are on Facebook. I set up a Facebook page myself and I still don't get it! There's nothing to do but find old or new friends, then write and read updates about other people. This is what my kid wants to do for hours every night? I don't get it. I feel like I am just wasting my time.*

Thankfully, for this generation of young people, time spent finding, connecting, and updating with other people is not wasted time. Can these trends for friends beat out decades of consumerism? Teenagers will answer that question if you're listening. They will tell you not to bet against hobbits saving the world.

It has always been both a fearful and a hopeful thought to realize that adults have the power not just to mentor or meet the desires of young people, but also to actually and perhaps permanently *form* the desires of young people. By engaging, guiding, punishing, and rewarding our children as they grow, we are not just teaching them what the world is like ("People do whatever they can to be better than other people"), but we are also teaching them what in the world is worth liking ("Money, even if it doesn't bring happiness, is essential in today's world, the more the better"). We are modeling what material things and human experiences are worth working and longing for. It is incorrect and dangerous to think that we adults are called only to mentor adolescents in their exercise of desire, as if we are spectators cheering for a certain outcome. Instead, the words of teenagers prove that they are also looking for help in the formation process of their desires. We are not mere witnesses to the unfolding adult in every young person, but instead we can be powerful part-authors of their spiritual wants and hopes.

Too often the kinds of questions that are asked in our self-help culture are: "Am I happy?" or "Am I satisfied?" I talk to many teenagers who ask themselves these questions all the time, but they are unsure of what their answer is—or what it should be. As one teenage girl put it, "I am not happy. Is anyone? I think I know what happy is, but don't know how *to get* to happy." Deeper and more liberating questions are: "Why do I want the things or experiences I want?" "Where did my wants come from?" "Do my desires represent magnets drawing me toward worthy treasures or are they in fact pulling me off-course, away from true and meaningful living?" So the question "Am I happy?" represents a moment not only to evaluate our state of satisfaction, but also to take an inventory of our desires and try to figure out where they come from. Adolescent feelings of unhappiness or lack of fulfillment can be a function of malformed desire. As adults, we take part in the shaping of their hearts and must therefore take responsibility for some of the directions of their passion. Adults cannot help young people to reorient their desires toward freedom and joy until we admit that we are in fact agents in their formation. So many of the world's great religious traditions share the teaching that the wise and joyful person does not so much *follow* his heart as *form* it critically, compassionately, and continually. Joy is not just a matter of finding what you want. It is a matter of wanting things and experiences that are liberating.

Until adults accept the reality that we play an enormous role in forming not only our own desires but those of our children, we cannot chart a course of parenting, teaching, or mentoring that is transformative or liberating for them or for ourselves. When I listen to young people speak of their desires for the future, it is clear that they have been taught for which prizes they should seek and for what values they should be prepared to sacrifice. In many cases, I am inspired by the longings that have been nurtured in them—"Without a soul life would be terribly different because there would be no passion"—and in others, I am distressed by their desires for wealth, popularity with a clique, and social power—"It's all about who you know." These are less signs of the innate desires of teenagers than they are transcripts of the adults who are talking and modeling around them. Teens are watching how and why we live and love. At every moment, we are teaching them what the world is and what they should want and work for in it. We teach them to seek their dreams passionately but we do not talk to them about whether or not these dreams are worthy of them or true to their set of gifts and skills. As one very competitive but anxious senior boy confessed, "I have very little idea where I am going in life, but I sure am going fast."

When asking young people what high school has been like for them and what it has taught them about life, I operate with the assumption that finishing high school should be a joyful accomplishment, and college, for those who can afford it, should provide at least as much excitement as uncertainty. But it is hard to find a sense of contentment or accomplishment among teens in any income bracket. About 20 to 30 percent of the highly successful seniors I have spoken to state that they do not know if they want to go to college at all. The same students also say, "But of course I'll go because I'm afraid not to." We have raised them to want college, but not all of our adolescents have been given the time or space to envision what college might be like. Movies and television depict the college experience as a collage of binge drinking, casual sex, exclusive social cliques, and dramatic relationships. Is it any wonder that a senior might question whether or not the traditional residential college reality is the kind of environment essential to a happy or fulfilling life? We may be so eager to get our children into a prestigious college that we are neglecting our role to first help form their hopes and moral expectations for what higher education can be. One male lacrosse student was talking to me after his practice and joked out loud: "I just visited a college last weekend on a recruiting visit and I am still laughing because if my parents had any idea what a 24/7 party college is going to be, they would never let me leave home!"

Adolescent angst about leaving high school, where we find it, begs the question why so many teenagers are confused about the meaning and purpose of their lives, the content of their character, or the inventory of their gifts. Why do they feel so fearful of the future and so exhausted from the stress of expectations from those who love them, when the reality of their situation is often bursting with gifts, resources, or opportunities? We cannot explain away this stress and anxiety by simply calling it immaturity. Look at very young children. Their tendency to smile or cry is natural, predictable, and mostly in sync with the world around them. Very young children often blurt out in public the raw reality of a situation; their reaction or language might be extreme or embarrassing, but often there is truth in their inconvenient expressions. Likewise, if our eighteen-year-olds are smiling or crying at the world, why would we dismiss them by saying they do not understand the world? Teens may not have the final word on what the adult world is actually like, but they certainly tell us about the world as they understand it. Whether a teenager's moral and spiritual life is a result of the adult world or just his or her flawed perception should be irrelevant to her teachers and mentors. Many young people say that their number one reason for disengaging with adults in conversation about meaning and purpose is because they (rightly, in my view) discerned that the adult set out in the conversation to correct the adolescent's view of the world instead of listening to it and engaging it. When adults practice perception-correction as a response to teenage talk, it is taken as rejection.

Instead of diagnosing teenagers as unable to know what is real or valuable, we might wonder instead why an otherwise joyful time in life—finishing high school—can be one of the darkest moments for an American teenager. The most credible, successful, and life-changing adult listeners to teens have given up labeling what teens say as wrong or right and instead honor their articulations as real perceptions. When I ask teens to describe the personalities or habits of adults whom they trust, they do not say that these adults "agree with me." In fact, rarely do students gravitate toward adults who simply agree with them, as their friends do. With adult relationships, teenagers are looking for something more. The number one description of an adult with whom teenagers want to engage is that he or she *listens*—in the words of adolescents, "lets me finish my sentences," "doesn't correct my speech," "doesn't judge me," or "lets me finish my stories." In fact, despite the worry of adults that they cannot or should not agree with young people, I cannot think of a teenager who has ever said to me that the reason an adult struck them as trustworthy or influential was because the adult "agreed" with the student. Teens, to their credit, are not looking for adults to be their friends. Teens are looking for formation.

I do not believe we can ignore adolescent frustration about the cruel competitiveness of the world around them or discount their negativity leaning toward nihilism as simply the complaints or misinformed fears of children. Adults are architects of the world surrounding every young person, and we cannot defensively tune out the criticisms of teenagers about the adult worlds of marriage, family, culture, or college. Faced with the sadness and the anger of teens about how violent, mean, and unfeeling the world appears to many of them at eighteen, it is tempting to defend ourselves by dismissing these gasps of adolescent angst as timeless teen rebellion, immaturity, selfish bitterness, or developmental inability to recognize the resources around them. Such dismissiveness will never get us closer to understanding the teenage heart and mind. After all, if someone swimming with you genuinely believes he is at that moment drowning, is it helpful to tell him he is wrong? Surely you would take hold of him and reassure him first, and only later talk about what is or is not a threat. It is the calling of adulthood and of teaching to aid teens in seeing reality, but to do so in light of the fact that all adolescents need rescue and a reassuring presence to begin any relationship with adults. The way to establish credibility and form relationships with teenagers is first to acknowledge that their perceptions are valuable and worthy of being heard, *even if incomplete.* We will never have the chance to mold the worldviews of teens (or, equally important, to have our own incomplete views of the world rounded out by adolescent perspectives) unless we first listen to their descriptions of the adult world they witness.

It is a fact that when teenagers speak of "the world," they refer mainly to their high school experience, their families, and a collection of other communities in which they spend time. Technology has also enabled a new generation of students to have more access to national and global news and events than ever before. I heard about the 1989 student protest in Tiananmen Square on the evening news, almost a day after it happened. In contrast, on the morning of September 11, 2001, a student in my classroom held up her Internet-enabled cell phone to show me a video feed from CNN of the World Trade Center towers on fire. Sitting at her desk and fixated on the two-inch screen, she then watched the towers fall. And then she watched it again and again and again. The Internet brings our teens deep into the world outside their high school halls and homes in ways unknown to any prior generation. This brings enormous challenges to adults who are trying to know and nurture their young people. Prior generations of parents had the luxury of having some idea of the potential truths and the traumas of an adolescent's day, but the World Wide Web can ensnare our young people with confusing or damaging images and ideas without our knowing that the wounds have been inflicted. Many parents give their children a cell phone so that they, the parents, have access to their children all day. But the price of this access is that the wide web of the world can reach those children as well.

That is why the talk of teens in this generation is harder to decode than any before: it is laced with words about the world that grow from experiences as personal and insular as their social clique but also as far-reaching as the newest fads in foreign lands, the juicy indiscretions of adults in other cultures, or the latest terrorist strike overseas. But despite the global reach of the technology that many teens hold in their own hands, I have found over the last decade that most adolescents, when they speak of the world, are still referring mostly to their personal lives at home or in high school. Teens still care more about their latest crush, who smokes, who got their driver's license, where the party is (and are they invited), or what colleges they will visit. Nothing on the Internet is more interesting than a handwritten note passed in math class.

Young people believe that high school is practice for the adult world and that its social rules and realities hint at the future of adult life. My students believe, on the whole, that the current heroes and villains in their high school culture will not cease their reign in college or beyond, but rather only tighten their grip on the levers of society. Ask a teenager why they are striving to be popular or thin or funny in high school and they will not say that they are trying to "get good at high school," but rather that they are trying to develop life skills that they believe adults need.

Though we would love for our young people to listen to us and to believe us when we speak positively and inspiringly about what the adult world will be like for them as they get older, it is an unavoidable fact that the world they *see* speaks for itself. In the world they see, a statistical majority of adults are obese, hypertensive, overworked, overconsuming, struggling with depression and anxiety, divorced or close to it, and financially indebted well beyond their means. Even if a young person is fortunate enough to find these statistical realities foreign to their own dinner tables, it only takes an email account, a Facebook page, a trip to any movie about American life, or a session with cable television to show them other and darker versions of the world waiting for them. The streaming media presentations of the brokenness of adult life on screens big and small pour ugly images and sad narratives of adult life into the eyes and souls of our teens. Year after year, it is harder and harder to find teenagers of any race, social class, or age who would describe American adults as healthy or happy. They all seem to know someone or a small group of adults who appear happy or at peace, but teens will remark how rare or odd these smiling grown-ups are in their world.

It might be good news that the television show teenagers watch most is not, for the first time in a decade, a "reality" television show. One of the most popular television shows in recent years for preteens and teens is called "Gossip Girl." But trust me: sit through an episode of these super-rich high school kids gone wild and you'll miss watching letter carriers or mortgage brokers eat bugs. "Gossip Girl" follows the extremely unreal lives of a group of millionaire teenagers living a Paris Hilton lifestyle while attending (rarely) an elite Manhattan private school. Drinking, cheating, backstabbing, casual sex, and designer drugs: you've seen this movie before. Students in my classes have asked for my thoughts on the moral issues (train wreck tales) in the series, so I went online and watched a dozen or so episodes. I went back to my students and said that the dialogue, sexual content, and other themes were completely over the top. What is interesting is that my students agreed. Many even called *all* of the characters in the show "pathetic," though entertaining. As a teacher, I was somewhat relieved that they were entertained but thankfully not engaged by the personalities of the show.

But what is, for me, the most deeply unsettling part of the show is the portrayal of parents. "Parents" would imply a level of maturity, self-mastery, and love that is mostly absent from the absurdly affluent adults that surround and corrupt the teen characters in "Gossip Girl." A show about sex-obsessed, mean girls with drinking problems and scruffy, bullying boys is not new, but the level of dysfunction, destructive choices, and bad influence of the adults *is* new. The ages of the adults portrayed put them among Generation Xers to Baby Boomers, and they display the worst spiritually bankrupt behavior ever attributed to either demographic. They change cars, bone structure, and spouses with the seasons. They sleep around with other parents of their own children's friends, and in one case, an always-out-of-town father leaves his Viagra for his son to "have a great prom night." What is so alarming is that when I ask students about the grown-ups in the series, they do not judge them nearly as harshly as they do the youth. The sense that adult life can be a bombing campaign with collateral damage on both adults and children does not seem over-the-top to present-day adolescents.

I cannot help thinking that teen anxiety about adult life has something to do with our presentation of it, either in reality or through the media. And it is not merely the fictional television shows or the real statistics of addiction, divorce, and financial chaos in the twenty-four-hour news cycle that crawls in front of

them on the bottom of every screen of their wired lives. The notion that adulthood is not to be envied is buried in every pharmaceutical commercial detailing the headache of finding the right
medications for even the most basic bodily functions, such as
sleeping, breathing, urinating, or having sex. So if adult life is
shown to be still more decades of the painful trial and error at
meaning that *is* adolescent life, with ever-increasing insecurity,
promiscuity, and failure, why shouldn't teens hunker down in the
bunker of their Internet bubble, barricade the door to adulthood
with a college keg, and disconnect from what they see marching
toward them with every birthday? After all, your television speaks
louder than you do.

In addition to the darkness that students see in the world that
awaits them, they feel incredibly rushed and stressed at the pace
of their lives right now. The very speed of middle-class life in this
country for a young person is unforgiving and unmanageable; as
one boy so aptly put it, "Nap time is over." Their talk of competition and seeking after achievement establishes that childhood, in
their view, is a race with winners and losers at the end of every
year, every season, every performance, or even at the close of every
day.

Not long ago, my HMO sent me down the road to a local hospital for a routine test. The hospital had a Level One Trauma Center, something I had never witnessed up close. In the span of the
morning and afternoon, emergency helicopters arrived, bringing
small explosions of activity and call-and-response scripts of life-
saving dialogue between those arriving and those receiving the
wounded.

What made this visit unique was that the dear friend waiting
with me was a medical doctor with years of experience in hospitals and emergency rooms. I peppered her with questions
throughout the day as the level of manic energy in the trauma
center went up and down. At one point a trauma victim who had
been in a car accident and suffered severe head and neck injuries
arrived by helicopter. As the trauma team roared by with half a
dozen different voices calling out numbers and the accident narrative, I leaned over to my friend and stated the obvious, "They
sure are in a hurry."

Without even looking up from her newspaper, she said softly, "Well, time is tissue." The phrase knocked every other existing thought out of me and I sat in silence. All I could do was repeat it back to her. *"Time is tissue?"*

"Yeah, that's what they say in emergency medicine." She turned the page of the newspaper. "That's the truth of the trauma center."

For years I have stood in the hallways of middle and high schools, as a teacher, coach, visitor, or consultant. Throughout all the frenzy in such scenes of American adolescent school life, I have harkened back to my afternoon in that trauma center, and again and again I hear that raw but honest description of the emergency room rule: *time is tissue.* That truth continues to haunt me because so much of middle and high school life apes the pressure and stress of a trauma center. How similar to emergency rooms our classrooms, practice rooms, sports fields, art rooms, and family dinner tables can become when the adults in charge of them do not sufficiently attend to the spiritual life and health of young people. It is our job to slow down and calm down the metabolism of daily life when it becomes manic or chaotic. Despite all the parenting books that talk about "equipping" or "training" your child to lead the pack of their peers or their generation, it is not our job to push our kids to "keep up" with the speed of American culture, as if that speed were a benign force or neutral state. Our homes and schools have doors to the outside world but there is a time to close them and to take control and responsibility for the care of souls in our midst. In hospitals, stressed and sleep-deprived but gifted professionals wait nervously at the always-open doors for the next arrival of a helicopter with a patient whose needs are urgent. But one has only to stand at the door of any competitive public or private high school in this country to witness parent after parent whose expectations of what the school can and should do to save their child from all pain and failure are beyond comprehension. We have let a culture of endless competition create a climate of mild but ambient crisis.

Too often our lives imitate the bustle and chaos of an emergency room, but with a mission that is much more ambiguous than saving lives. Perhaps it is time to refocus on our families and schools to be sure that we do not violate the wisdom of the Hippocratic principle—to "do no harm" to the spiritual lives of our young people. Hospital professionals rush to save lives, which is as it should be. Too often, parents, coaches, and schools rush to *perfect* lives, and this is *not* as it should be. One of the purposes of hospitals is to heal people so that they have more time—time to enjoy life and share it, to learn more, to love more, and to realize more fully the experience of being human. In this proper paradigm, the school and the family are the very places the hospital saves you to enjoy.

 *Chapter Three*

MINEFIELDS AND PLAYING FIELDS

Teenagers Listening to Us

"To be successful, someone else has to fail."

As I approached her locker that day, I saw the balloons and other decorations put up by friends to tell the world that it was her sixteenth birthday. It was an hour before school began, and she was alone at the locker looking unexpectedly sad. I wished her a happy birthday. She thanked me quietly with a momentary glance and fake smile. We knew each other well and, instantly curious why she seemed down on a day of impending celebration, I asked what could have caused a frown so early in the morning on her birthday. No details, just a shrug. I tried another approach, asking playfully what she did from the moment she got up. She reported in a monotone voice that she got up early, put on her favorite clothes, and met her mom at the table for a brief birthday breakfast with her younger brother. Her mom read aloud an email from her father, who was, as usual, out of town on business. And then, petting the locker decorations and pointlessly reorganizing her hanging jackets to look busy, she told me the birthday present her mother gave her: a subscription to Weight Watchers.

"Did you ask for that?" I said, trying not to jump to judgment and trying to understand how such a terrible idea for a present for a teenage girl came about. This teenage girl was not overweight at all, probably no more than 5 feet 2 inches tall and no more than a size 6 or 8 in women's clothing.

"No," the girl said without taking her eyes off the back of the locker. "Mom says she got one for herself too and that we can do it together." This otherwise well-adjusted and happy young person looked terribly sad at that moment, not to mention physically awkward, with her twisting hands, tapping feet, and blinking eyes, as if she hated being in every inch of her own body and was trying to squirm her soul out of it.

I remember wishing at that moment that I could be decades wiser or quicker with healing words. I wanted so much to know what to say, but I didn't. After a pause, she turned and looked right into my face. She popped a small but loud bubble with her habitual morning mint gum. I smiled and said the first thing that came out of my mouth. "I love your outfit. You picked awesome colors for a birthday." She looked down at the black-and-pink color theme that ran through her choice of hairband, shirt, pants, and socks, and then smiled with an artist's pride. "My best friend Ashley has the same shirt, so I am *totally* hoping she doesn't wear it today." Blood was coming back into her face. "Did Ashley do all this birthday decorating of your locker?" She nodded quickly, her face lit up, and she poured out all her thoughts about the loving gesture of her friends, and which pictures in the handmade collage I should (and should not) focus on. Her heart had begun to beat again as she pointed and narrated every sticker, photo, and colored ribbon. But I couldn't get the voice in my own head to stop: *What was her mother thinking?*

A decade later, I have a much better idea of what her mother was thinking. In fact, had I called up that mother (or the dozens like her I have met over the years), I can imagine the answers she would give to justify a mother-daughter subscription to Weight Watchers for a sixteenth birthday. The more I have witnessed of how parents are responding to the pressures of raising "successful" children, the more I understand the tactics they employ to help their children survive. I don't agree with a lot of those efforts, but I understand that parents are simply trying to do their best. I see what parents fear in the often unforgiving college admissions process or in the shrinking job market. I am sure the birthday mother loves her daughter dearly. Her gift was not thoughtless, and to assume it was thoughtless gets us no closer to understanding and helping the parent or the child in this scenario.

Since I care about both the mother and the daughter, I choose instead to consider that the gift *was* a thoughtful attempt to help the daughter succeed, however misdirected. I am sure that mother wanted to mark her daughter's rite of passage in turning sixteen by giving her a gift that proudly put aside the toys of childhood and treated her like a young woman. I am also sure the mother did in fact want to create some kind of shared experience for them—some journey to share together. In a social class where many of her adult peers had personal trainers and frequently gave gym memberships as gifts to spouses and even their own children, I am sure the Weight Watchers idea was just a version of the gifts-toward-self-improvement that are all too common among Baby Boomer parents and other demographics that worship social mobility. And I am sure that this mother saw her daughter's baby fat lasting perhaps a year or two longer than her peers. Knowing how cruel the world can be (though apparently unaware of how she colluded with its values), this mother had made the calculation that excess weight would be harshly teased or socially punished in high school, college, and beyond, so any hint of it should be addressed early. Her gift was an act of loving protection, a weapon against the world.

I have had many parents monopolize my ear at music performances or on the sidelines of games, worrying out loud about the excess weight of their round-faced children. I am not talking about obese children, which is a serious public health crisis in America, but about preteens and teens who are late in shedding baby fat or have rounder faces than their peers or struggle with acne that discolors their faces. Success-driven parents are concerned that the world of high school and beyond will find their children ugly and punish them for it, and perhaps they are correct in this prophecy. The impetus for patient and generous listening to even the most upsetting parents is the admission that the world can be, in fact, as cruel as their deepest fears envision. We may differ profoundly on how to respond to that world, but to ignore the empirical evidence that money or physical beauty empowers young people in this country is naïve and unhelpful—whether we are talking to teens or their parents.

Rather than accept the timeless physical awkwardness of adolescence, many parents instead begin to intervene with hopes of saving their son or daughter from social suffering. This desire to rescue is understandable, but many young people resent this intervention:

> It won't be my life until I move out of my house.
> My mom is a slave-driver.
> I have no privacy.
> My parents say the world is cruel but they can dish it out to
>   each other 24/7.
> My father is a control maniac.

It is not that teens prefer to suffer alone, but they distrust the parental motivations behind the rescue. The teen outrage comes when the child finds out that the intervention is as much if not entirely aimed at preserving popularity or external beauty, rather than to improve self-esteem as an end in itself. Weight is a good example of this. It is one thing to intervene, rightly, when a child is obese. But when a teenage girl receives a subscription to Weight Watchers for being simply rounder than her peers or heavier than other students in her social clique, then it is clear that the intervention is to invest in notions of popularity or material success under the guise of improving health. Parents, often behind the backs of their children, problem-solve against weight, acne, or any other blemishes that they observe to be a threat for future success. Remarks overheard in the parking lot or from the sidelines often run like this: "We know our son's basically healthy and happy, but those rolls on his gut aren't getting smaller"; "My wife looked like that at her age too and grew out of it, thank God"; "He's built just like his grandfather, but we hope it goes away"; "We're just praying that his travel team this summer will help that baby fat disappear." It increases our sense of potency as adults when we can afford to intervene against the struggles of adolescence. But the teens I talk to wait daily to see whether or not their parents or teachers stand up to the distorted values of the world rather than obey them. They are waiting for us to be heroes, not uncritical coaches or generous patrons for equipping children to be popular and successful in a materialistic society.

The sad face of the birthday girl I saw in the hallway was the result of an understandable but no less tragic desire of the mother to perfect, not protect her daughter. Though it is easy to criticize the mother for being preoccupied with her daughter's weight, she is nonetheless correct in her cultural analysis: skinniness sells, beauty matters, and the world can be cruel to those who lack luster. To deny these sad metrics for value in our contemporary culture is naïve and worse, will disqualify an adult as intelligent or helpful in the eyes of an adolescent. It is, however, our ultimate vocation as parents to challenge prevailing notions of worth and beauty where they are narrow or cruel, not to participate in them with the defense that we are just trying to help our children succeed. Our work and intervention as adults should instead be to construct and support a child's inner life, to fill them with authentic truths about their immutable dignity and worth. While we focus on removing their blemishes, many students feel like we are missing their inner strengths and inner needs:

> *If my mom knew what my friends think about me, she'd see that I'm really not a lost cause.*
> *I wish my dad could see me in chemistry lab—I'm actually really good at stuff . . . and I do know how to clean up after myself.*
> *Why is everything about me a problem?*

Teens need us to rescue them from the world's shallowness, not teach them to swim in it.

I often ask teenagers to give me one word to describe what it is like to be a teenager. Most of the time they come back with adjectives that capture the uncertainty of this period of life, such as "wild," "complicated," or "confusing." More often the adjectives are dark or sad, like "painful," "lonely," or "stressful." My favorite over the last decade has come up only occasionally but by a wide variety of students who always deliver it in more or less the same way. The student pauses at my question, and then with a loud sigh says, "Ouch!" I can remember a particular first-generation Asian student who smiled after choosing it and then added "Yeah...'ouch'...that word says it all. 'Ouch' basically sums up my life since I started shaving." We laughed together. But I wanted to be clear about his point. "So are you saying that the *shaving* hurts?" He didn't look at me, but only gently ran his hand along his face from the ear down to his not-smiling mouth. "Trust me, shaving is the least painful thing about being a teenager."

A mature and creative twelfth-grade girl also shared a memorable conversation about her word. "Ouch...that's it. That's my word for being a teenager: Ouch." She nodded her head at the end of her sentence as if to underline her choice. This self-taught guitarist had been bubbly and noisy in middle school, but had become more quiet and serious during her senior year as her older brother prepared to go to war in Iraq. "Is 'ouch' a word you use a lot when you talk about your life these days?" I asked. She bit her lower lip tentatively. "Well, now that you ask....I never actually *use* the word 'ouch.' It's more like the sound my heart makes these days. And not just these day, actually, but kind of since high school started. It's sort of like the sound my life makes." I thought I understood the main source of her pain. When I brought up her brother and the war, she voiced her fears about his deployment, but was quick to add, "Everybody I know is worried or hurting about something. Since I started telling people about my freaking out about my brother, I have heard a thousand crazy situations my friends are dealing with, you know? It's like we're all on the edge."

Whether it is the actual physical growing pains that irritate and exhaust teenage bodies, or the constant shifts in the social landscape that scrape the heart each day, or catastrophic events like divorce or death, every teenager is battling with pain and grief. However, pain is rarely the ruling feeling in teenagers each day. Spend any time with teens and it is clear that they have an ability to mix passion, joy, and inspiration with emotional or social frustration and pain.

Bookstores burst with the works of experts of one kind or another documenting the utter depths of teen despair that manifest in self-injury, addiction, and suicide. These rare but tragic tales of teens suffering or even dying from forms of depression or mental illness are not what I mean when I say that all teenagers are in pain. I am not trying to stretch the extreme suffering of some young people and suggest that every teenager is on the edge of addiction, self-injury, or suicide. The Internet is filled with books and blogs on parenting that too often traffic in tales of the darkest narratives of unhealthy and unhappy teens. Fear sells. Adults are afraid for every aspect of the life of their teenagers, and the piles of published works describing worst-case scenarios and rescue tactics form a dark and growing forest that justifies their sense of dread. If you believe everything you read about Internet stalkers, the rise of illicit drugs, the pandemic of bullying, or the sexual activity of children and preteens, you might not ever let your child out of your house. Despite our confidence in our ability to speak freely and honestly to our kids, the unfortunate truth is that what our children are picking up from us is a contagious sense of fear. According to teens, our actions teach them to fear losing or failing in every venue of their lives.

These same fears about the immediate safety and ultimate career and life success of our teens are clouding our capacity to discern and discuss the more subtle daily feelings and thoughts of our teenagers. We can become so worried about what they *might* tell us that we are not listening carefully to what they are actually saying. As a result, teens suspect that adults are more afraid of the extremes than they are interested in their daily lives. As one boy told me, he wanted his parents to ask and care more about "the stuff in between the stuff." Most teens I know move back and forth between pain and pleasure not as extreme poles, but rather in a confusing mix of both feelings. Teenagers know that adults are watching the outcomes and the extremes of their experiences, but they long to be asked about the details in between the deadlines and the sidelines. While we wait anxiously for them to achieve either success or failure, they are looking for our non-anxious companionship as they are tossed about in the whitewater rapids of adolescent experiences in between the starts and stops of each day. As one boy said to me, "I got home from the game last night and my dad asked the same question he's asked since I was in Little League: 'Who won?' But I actually had the funniest and coolest conversation ever with my coach on the bus going home. I don't think my dad has ever asked me about a bus ride in my life."

A student came to me on the first day of school armed with over a hundred pictures to show me of his summer family vacation to the Grand Canyon. Charlie was not usually talkative and rarely engaged adults, so I gave him the space to share every detail. When I asked him to show me his favorite picture, he dug to the bottom of the pile to pull out a photo already more worn and smudged than any other. In the picture he was standing on a piece of sandy desert land with his feet spread apart and trying unsuccessfully to look serious and pensive, his hand cupping under his chin, posing as Rodin's *Thinker*. I recognized the site as the Four Corners Monument, where Arizona, New Mexico, Utah, and Colorado come together at a marked point that lets you stand in four states at once. "How cool is *that*!" he yelled, and playfully slammed his hand on the picture as if he were throwing down a winning poker hand.

I smiled and then pulled out my MP3 recorder because Charlie loved to make recordings of his creative thoughts. "So," I whispered and leaned the microphone toward him as if he were a celebrity, "what *did* it *feel* like to stand in four states at once?" He smiled broadly and paused for the right words. "Crazy! It felt crazy. I mean, it's just a piece of ground. You wouldn't know what it is now if there wasn't this monument thing there. Instead of feeling like four states, it felt like maybe those lines were just made up! It just felt crazy, like unreal, like maybe states don't really exist and maybe things don't *actually* start and stop the way people say. I mean, it was just a piece of dirt before somebody said it was something else." He then took a breath, slowed down, and became more calm and thoughtful about his words. "The whole thing made me start to think that maybe the edges of things are not real, you know, like, we just tell ourselves things to get around the world but that those things aren't totally real, you know? It's like that NASA picture of the Earth from space. There are no state lines at all." He picked up the picture and spoke to it. "It kind of felt like I was standing on my life, you know? Like this crazy intersection of all this different stuff and stress happening at once to one person—like my body is some kind of intersection for things too big to touch at more than one point. It's like people draw these serious lines and states and call the lines real so that the bigness of things is less scary, but when you actually stand there, you realize the lines don't mean anything except to the people who drew them. But once somebody draws the lines and tells you what it means to be where you are, you start to feel crazy because it doesn't mean the same thing for you. I feel like I look at me from space and everybody else looks at me on a map."

As I have wandered for years through libraries, bookstores, and websites searching for resources to understand teenagers, I have come to believe we are a society more interested in the extremes of human experiences than the pathways from one stage of life to another: the left versus right in politics, the rags to riches in television dramas, the innocent made victim by betrayal in fiction, or the absolute good against the absolute evil in blockbuster films. Ask teenagers about how adults measure worth in the world and they will tell you that we teach and preach our moral lessons in extremes. I once showed the 2005 multimillion-dollar movie *Gladiator* to a group of students. I paused the film to explain the ancient tradition of the Roman emperor putting his thumb up or down to determine the fate of the last competitors standing in the Coliseum. At the end of my brief explanation, one hard-working boy from India looked at me and said, "Why do you call that idea 'ancient?'"

I spent an afternoon with high schoolers at a reception that followed the funeral of one of their parents. The moods swings over the three or four hours we spent on a patio from dusk to late into the night were a primer on the wide spectrum of adolescent emotional capacity. The boy who lost his father was understandably teary on and off, falling into silence during group talks far more often than he ever had. I sat with him, two girls, and two other boys in his grade for hours while they told stories, periodically stood up in pairs to shoot baskets, did impressions of teachers or celebrities, occasionally broke into songs from Disney movies, sat on each other's laps, discussed the meaning of death, family, and love, and rested their heads on each other's shoulders until everyone's heads were nodding off in exhaustion. This group of adolescents performed the holy task of accompanying a friend who had lost his dad with the grace of any group of grown-ups. All the borders of adult-established lines for appropriate and inappropriate grief expressions faded with the sun at twilight; that is, they were not afraid to play within five minutes of crying. They were more interested in loving each other than in "saying the right things." The mood froze, however, whenever an adult walked over, expressed condolences, and reminded them "what had happened." At those moments when an adult reminded the teenagers where they were on the maps of adult perception, they looked as dazed as the teenage traveler to Four Corners who said to me, "It felt crazy." Perhaps the adults were wondering or even disapproving of how a group of teenagers could play tag, charades, or name-that-Disney-tune loudly within just hours of a parent's burial. My abiding thought throughout that evening in my plastic patio chair was that the fellowship of these young people was doing more to heal them that night than could any adult watching them nervously from behind window glass.

It would be hard for someone of any age to be marooned on an island with just a few others, whether it was Golding's island in *Lord of the Flies* or one on a television reality show. Very quickly you would learn to fear those around you if you came to think that your peers knew more or cared more about how to win than how to work with one another. In experiences where we feel safe, such as in loving relationships or when we are learning or even vacationing, many of us get in touch with our gifts, talents, and potential contributions to others. When we are afraid, we instinctively fall back on assessing dangers, fearfully aware of our imperfections, weaknesses, and liabilities. It is our environment— or more accurately, our perception of our safety in that environment—that often determines what kind of inventory we take of ourselves, and how compassionate or cruel that inventory is. Fear breeds a sense of immediacy and inadequacy. When afraid, we do not take comfort in the promise of our potential or in the power of our gradually enfolding gifts. In crisis, competence is more important than character; it becomes the coin of the realm. Weakness points down the path toward failure or victimization.

The adolescents we will encounter in this section demonstrate the clear connection between their perceptions of the world as harsh or unsafe and their resulting perceptions of self that are critical, unforgiving, and uncertain of their worth. In addition to the negative words teens use to describe their own lives, it is also clear that they often feel ashamed for the morally problematic survival skills they have adopted. When adolescents perceive a *Lord of the Flies* world, where every peer is to another a wolf, they are driven more by self-defense than by self-discovery.

Most teens I know—despite their words or deeds to the contrary—sincerely want to appear as if their lives are working and successful. Teenagers want to please the adults around them. Though few teens I know have the words to describe the phenomenon, most have a keen sense of the parenting pattern of Generation X and Baby Boomer parents. The most common pattern is what psychologists call "operant conditioning." This is a method of forming people by responding to their decisions or actions with punishments or rewards aimed to incentivize certain outcomes, as opposed to what is called "classic conditioning," which involves planting desires in the first place. Operant conditioning as a parenting habit attempts to shape the child's allocations of energy and talent by showering love for the outcomes we want and subtly shaming unwanted outcomes with silence or withdrawal. I asked a student when he would complete an assignment for my class to interview a parent about his or her views of immigration. "Well, I have a soccer game today. I'll see my dad tonight for dinner and hanging out if we win our game," said the sophomore boy. "But if we lose, he'll probably go back to the office for the night and I won't see him."

More than any generation of young people in recent history, these teens want to play along with the games put before them and they want to please the adults who are watching. Teens appear to know instinctually that many Baby Boomer and Generation X parents define their own worth by the outputs of their children. But the combination of unrealistic expectations, conditional love, and the need to beat out their friends and peers in the Darwinian ditch of college preparatory high school life causes many adolescents to fake health, happiness, or investment in the paths and performances prescribed by their parents. The result of wanting to win at whatever path toward success is laid before them often causes teens to mask their uncertainties, their fears, and their failures. I recently read Andre Agassi's personal memoir of his life in tennis and was stunned to read that he hated tennis because it was forced upon him by his father. But Agassi felt he had no choice as a child, so he accepted his fate and the only path to affirmation that his father offered. Agassi hid his lack of desire for tennis until his retirement from the sport. But this façade was difficult to maintain, and brought bouts of depression, aggression, and even periodic drug use (such as crystal meth) throughout his adolescent and adult life.

At a time when teenage brains and bodies are crying out to be discovered for all the new powers and pulses that erupt in adolescence, teens are aware of unrealistic or inauthentic parental expectations and take the journey to self-discovery under duress and fear of failure. They are often more afraid of who they are than inspired by who they might become. In the words of one wise young woman, "We are uncomfortable with who we really are."

It is our job as adults to help our kids mature into morally and spiritually healthy people. But too often parents and teachers reward or punish only the external lives or marketable outcomes of teens, training them to ignore or abandon their own inner lives and focus their attention instead on the things that matter to the adults around them. To assuage our fears that our kids will not be competitive, we unfortunately teach them to fear themselves. Adolescence becomes a high-stakes game of learning what adults want and dream, not a personal journey for the teenager to get to know his or her own passions and goals. The result of this adult-modeled idolatry for external productivity and cultural celebrity is that students are unable to be peacefully or patiently fair in their self-analysis. Many teens I teach have mostly given up on finding what they desire. They instead try to figure out what adults want them to do.

It is a myth that teens are self-absorbed. This notion does not hold up in actual conversations with teens. The teenagers I talk to across the country are strangers to their own passions; they play recklessly with their lives not out of a commitment to fulfill their desires, but out of a need to deaden their fears or escape from a growing sense that they are being catapulted toward adult lives with no inner connection to or investment in that trajectory. Today's teens are not James Dean in *Rebel Without a Cause*; these teenagers have become *more* dependent on adults from childhood into adolescence, not less. They try hard to discover what is wanted *for* them rather than to discover their own passions. This kind of parenting is replication, not formation. And the rush to keep up with these imposed plans for their lives sidelines the development of the habits of the teenage heart—dreaming, discerning, learning, and moral courage. The rushed teen hushes mystery and seeks means to survive and please; addiction to adult affirmation stunts their growth and narrows their outlook. We all know these striving teens who mistake arrogance for confidence, manipulation for creativity, and achievement for maturity. Many teenagers are all too aware of this, and when discussing the meaning of death, family, and love they grieve deeply for the esteem, spontaneity, safety, pride, and freedom they felt as children.

Verbatim responses written by twelfth-grade girls
in answer to this question:
"Tell me things that are TRUE about YOU."

I am always wanting more, never satisfied.
I want to live according to my morals, but I am scared that
    at college I won't.
I am SO not ready to go to college.
I gossip.
I always have to be right.
I have no idea what I want to be when I grow up.

I'm always afraid to fail.
I don't feel at home anywhere.
I say things I don't mean.
I'm addicted to working out and trying to become perfect.
I'm just so tired . . . always.
Grown-ups are totally screwed up.
All of my possessions turn into obsessions.
I love my family intensely but sometimes I forget to show it.
I need constant reassurance.
I am sensitive and easily hurt, but I don't tell people.
I physically cannot be alone, it terrifies me.
I am too self-centered.
I have to let out my feelings if I am mad. I won't be calm until my feelings are expressed.
I am not truly happy, I don't know how to change it, but I haven't been happy for a while. I mask my unhappiness behind my smile.
I want to be honest with my parents but I can't get up the courage to tell them how I really feel.
I have a pretty bad and quick temper.
Everything I do, good or bad, is calculated. I am not impulsive at all.
I have mastered lying and cheating. I hate it, but it's my instinct at this point.
I suck at relationships . . . a lot . . . I guess it's genetic.
I love my best friends as much if not more than myself.
I am really proud of myself that I did not turn out like my mom. I love her but she doesn't love herself.
I'm afraid I haven't appreciated my dad enough.
I'm horrible with money.
I can't accept praise without doubting it.
I can be too self-centered.
When I get criticism, I start doubting my abilities.
I wish I could go back to the innocence of childhood.
It's hard for me to make friends, and I feel really lonely sometimes.
I compare myself to others all the time.
I want to be comfortable with who I am.

I love her, but I don't think my mother really accepts who I am.

I love my friends more than they will ever know. They are my true home.

I bottle my emotions. For once in my life, I really want to be able to say exactly what I feel inside. That's not my life though—most of the time when I'm angry, I just don't speak or I smile and fake it.

I am a really good liar because people don't really expect it of me.

I don't work hard but I still do well, I'm worried what will happen when I'm faced with something that requires me to try. I'm not sure if I have the work ethic to get it done.

I lie to get out of trouble... but it makes me sooo nervous. But school has taught us to lie.

I worry way too much. I wish I could just relax and have more faith.

I'm really bad at sharing with other people (material things or ideas).

I want to be perfect even though I know it's not possible.

What I do is never enough for myself.

I like eliminating my competition.

Verbatim responses written by twelfth-grade boys
in answer to this question:
"Tell me things that are TRUE about YOU."

I lie because I fear that nobody will like the real me.

I don't know if I actually want to go to college.

I am really, really self-conscious.

I rely on technology to survive.

I am not ready for college.

I have little self-confidence.

I'm very competitive.

I leave everything to the last minute.

*I need friends and people around me . . . loneliness is the
scariest thing to me.*

I hope I learn to treat women better than my father does.

*As a guy, I am socially awkward and uncomfortable around
girls.*

*I act mellow and laid-back, but I am paranoid and a little
crazy all the time.*

*I hate school. The only reason I continually try in school is
to make my parents satisfied, not to make them
happy . . . that would be impossible.*

I am scared about growing up and becoming an adult.

I have to hear or play music every day.

I enjoy food more than I enjoy going to church.

I have very little idea where I'm going in life.

*I probably should have focused more on grades and less on
video games.*

I lie and always say what people want to hear.

*Yesterday I learned more about one of my closest friends
than I had ever before, and now I'm wondering what
else I don't know.*

*I always plan the rest of my life out—because I'm afraid of
not having anything to do.*

I'm friends with people I don't like, especially girls.

I need to be around friends to be happy.

I find the unknown terrifying.

*I can be compassionate but I am equally capable of being
inconsiderate.*

*I'm conscious about my future and that I need to do well in
school so that I can live comfortably.*

I'm scared of dying.

I'm gay and get tired of hiding.

I analyze EVERYTHING.

Sometimes I don't even trust myself.

Music is my savior.

I want to be a good person.

*I can be very mean, selfish, and unappreciative of my
family.*

I care too much about what others think.

I don't show people how I am really feeling.
I am always tired.
I depend way too much on my parents. I need to be more of
*   an individual.*
I can't focus for more than 20 minutes.
I'm materialistic and care about my appearance.

In the previous chapter, we saw what truths and trends teenagers witness around them and what they are learning about how the adult world works, including the mixed messages about meaning, dignity, and relationships that come from adults and from the media. The anxieties that greet them at sunrise and haunt them at the end of each day cause many adolescents to feel emotionally unsafe, physically unable, intellectual unprepared, spiritually unknown, and conditionally loved:

I am always wanting more, never satisfied.
I am just so tired.
I say things I don't mean.

Teens are all too aware that the adults around them—perhaps more than any prior generation of parents in America—are nervously watching them around the clock, engineering each child's life toward material success and ready to immediately intervene at any scent of possible failure: "Everything I do, good or bad, is calculated." An eighteen-year-old boy I talked to in a private school near Tacoma, Washington, describes with wonder a brief respite he enjoyed in a family that is hyperfocused on seeking success and avoiding failure:

We went on a safari once as a family and I loved it. We never knew what we would see from minute to minute. We never knew where we were going next or what would happen. But no one was stressed. Everything felt like enough—like more than enough. We just got excited to see what would happen next. But at home, nothing is enough. And everyone is stressed out waiting to see what will happen next.

For all this adult scrutiny and watchfulness, however, many teens I talk to do not feel as if adults are actually listening to them or getting to know them as individual people. They report feeling watched but not known, herded but not heard. All too aware of the fears of their parents, teens wonder out loud if any adult knows of their own adolescent fears:

> *I act mellow and laid-back, but I am paranoid.*
> *I find the unknown terrifying.*
> *I'm always afraid to fail.*
> *I physically cannot be alone, it terrifies me.*
> *I'm scared of dying.*

One senior boy I interviewed at a school in Pennsylvania said it this way:

> *My parents are only interested in stuff that happens to me or that I do—good or bad. They don't ever ask about just being alive, you know? Like, the being alive in between the stuff. But then again, I don't hear them talking about anything in their lives that way either, so I guess they wouldn't know what I mean.*

Adults are seen by many teens to be more worried than wondering, more critical than curious, more invested than interested, and more judgmental than joyful:

> *When I get criticism, I start doubting my abilities.*
> *I compare myself to others all the time.*
> *I love her, but I don't think my mother really accepts who I am.*
> *I lie and always say what people want to hear.*

The adolescents I meet *want* to talk about their experience of the world (not just how they are succeeding or struggling in it) and they *want* to process the accumulating lessons they are learning and, at times, the wounds they are getting:

> *I bottle my emotions.*
> *For once in my life, I really want to be able to say exactly what I feel inside.*
> *I want to be honest with my parents but I can't get up the courage to tell them how I really feel.*

Students in school after school I have visited state that conversations with their parents have a limited, bifocal pattern of inquiry—what they call "only looking forward and backward." Adults in their lives appear mostly interested in scrutinizing the past for blame (a B-minus on a test) and mining the future for opportunities of success (a summer internship in Chile). Teens are perplexed at this relentless line of questioning from parents that looks back to seek explanations for failure: "What happened in biology today?" "Did you use the flashcards I bought you?" "Did you win the game last night?" "Did you get a good start on that outline at the library yesterday?" Similarly, teens are frustrated with the line of questioning that ignores the pains or uncertainties of the present moment to skip forward to the ways to ensure success in the future: "Are you going to go for extra help tomorrow in math class?" "Did you at least land a speaking role in the play?" "It's already January, have you started looking for a summer job?" What is lost in these conversations that only look back for answers or forward for future opportunities is any evidence that the adult cares about the teenager's experience and feelings in the *present.* Consequently, we begin to create a restlessness with the present for our young people. Because we do not sit patiently with them and express curiosity about their lives today, acknowledging what is going on inside them, teenagers actually become uncomfortable in the present themselves. We have made the present a lonely place where adults and their love are absent. This anxiety leads to self-doubt and results in so many of the self-descriptions in this chapter.

In our rush to get information or to lead our kids to lessons from their own lives, we also teach them that rushing is an acceptable way to process emotions as an adult. But students are quick to mourn the experiences of their own lives that are lost in the race of everyday life:

> *I leave everything to the last minute.*
> *I'm just so tired.*
> *I love my family intensely but sometimes I forget to show it.*
> *I am always behind.*

What I do is never enough for myself.
There is never enough time for anything.

Most teenagers I know want to be better friends, siblings, students, and children, but when I ask them why they cannot reach their goals to deepen relationships and practice loyalty and forgiveness, they universally respond that they have no time for pursuits that are not measured by trophies or transcripts. As one wise African-American senior wrote on a survey about how and when adults have supported her, "If it's not graded, it's not guided."

Given that I know how proud most parents are of their children, I am amazed when I see those same students so doubtful of their worth and potential. Clearly, we are saving our supportive words only for the beginning or end of games or performances. And when I ask students why they do not share more of their emotions with their parents, many respond with some version of "that's not the kind of stuff my parents ever ask about." The tragedy of these patterns of family talk is that many teens observe in them a sidelining of emotions by adults, and the lesson learned is that one's present emotional state, whatever it may be, is less important than the schedule for success of the day, week, or year. Over time, teens adapt and internalize these patterns in their own relationships: "Yesterday I learned more about one of my closest friends than I had ever before, and now I'm wondering what else I don't know." The reality is that young people learn how and for what to be curious from adults. That is how we reveal our values and the values of the world outside our families and schools. Part of the overwhelming responsibility of parenting and teaching is how much we contribute to the patterns of curiosity and methods of measurement that our children develop internally and that they will use to define and judge themselves throughout life.

Many teens at the end of high school have already developed the habit of sidelining their emotions to pursue success; they are more comfortable talking about their goals than their gut feelings. I was having lunch with a boy during the summer after his junior year in high school. We were meeting to talk about ideas for his college essays that he would write in the coming September. He had always been a champion wrestler, but in the prior year he had sustained a serious shoulder injury in the first week of the season that sidelined him for the rest of the year. As a result of his injury his chances of being recruited by a college athletic program were severely reduced; he might need future surgeries and might never compete at the same level again. Consequently, he and his parents needed to "make serious changes" to the list of colleges to which he would apply.

Hearing of his situation, I volunteered to meet him at a chili restaurant for lunch on a hot August day, with hopes to get him excited about a new list of colleges that did not require him to be a great wrestler for admission. This otherwise energetic student was passive and mournful that day, which was to be expected. I had taught him and cheered for him in years of competitions. But every time I tried to get him to express some emotion about his change of fortune over lunch, he grabbed a bag of oyster crackers from the pile of free packs on the table. He would squeeze the bag hard until it popped, turning every cracker to dust. He went through eight or ten bags while we talked. In another kind of conversation, I would have perhaps suggested he not waste the crackers in this way, but it was clear that such externalizing was making a small but real difference in his ability to say something about his pain.

In between the sound of exploding cracker bags, I asked how he felt about his injury. "Whatever. Shit happens." How did he feel about his need to find new colleges? "I don't want to go to any of the colleges on my dad's new list. . . . The only thing I know about them is that I have heard of them." Had he and his parents talked about actually visiting new colleges? "It doesn't matter whether I see them or not. I've just got to suck it up. . . . My parents say we can still save this thing." What did he want to study at college? "I don't know." Then he sat back against the wood bench in our booth, puzzled, as if I'd asked an inappropriately difficult question for a chili lunch. He was intelligent enough (and probably coached at length already for such questions in college interviews) to be instantly aware that he should have the answer, and waited long enough to go through all the right answers in his head, but then: "Honestly," he said in a huge exhale, "I'm actually kinda tired of school. So, like, whatever. I'll do whatever the school is good at . . . I guess."

It was a sincere answer. Like so many boys I have known, this young man had been trained more *to be coached* than to be creative, trained to respond rather than to initiate, trained to follow the leader rather than write the script. But in his case, the adult authors of his success story could not keep an injury out of the plot, so now they were trying to "save this thing" and get him into a college sight-unseen that at least people "had heard of," ready to major in whatever his college put before him. I know he was in terrible pain to lose the joy of wrestling. But none of the adults in his life were talking about his grief. All the conversations were a kind of damage control, a rescue effort to find a prestigious-enough college that would take this boy without athletic deals. But his feelings were as far from his awareness and understanding as from mine, and I left lunch convinced that only the oyster crackers had a sense of what he really felt.

Teenagers more familiar with parental plans than with their own passions have no inner compass to find a new direction when their parents' plans fall through. Their own passions are often a mystery to teenagers and therefore unable to light new paths and plans. One reason teens get so involved in their hobbies (music, tattoos, video games) is that overly involved parents have set the vocational course for the child from an early age in almost everything else. Thus they are able to express their personal passions and choose their own directions only on the margins of their scheduled days. Since the "success" plans come from adults from whom they seek love, moreover, teens understandably have a hard time questioning these imposed ideas or intruding with their own ideas when they differ from adults. Teens are afraid of appearing to reject the parent who has wrapped loving inside coaching and established intimacy as a reward for achievement.

But finding and practicing a passion is a very different process when adolescents are away from parents and coaches. I have shared community service projects to clean parks or build houses with students and joined their teams for field-day games of egg tosses, three-legged races, or water balloon fights. Mistakes and bloopers among teens in their own games bring laughter, bonding, hugs, and high-fives of support and affirmation from peers. Students rejoice in their cluelessness about how to use a circle saw or outdoor generator; they put themselves in each other's hands while water rafting or mountain climbing, not fearing dependency, but rather practicing it with shy smiles and openness to intimacy. When the scoreboards and camcorders are absent, students enjoy the equalizing effects of imperfection and welcome the opportunities where need breeds participation and problem solving. When students are not performing for adults—either in successful acts or in destructive acts of rebellion—I am amazed at their playfulness, support for one another, and acceptance of failure.

The opportunity to mature is lost to students who are petrified that failure will weaken the bonds of love with adults. Such teens develop little sense that failures are part of life and might actually be sources of wisdom and growth. "I didn't get a part in the musical," a sophomore girl said to me with palpable sadness and feelings of rejection. "How do you feel about that?" I asked. "What difference does it make? The point is, now I have to quickly choose a sport this season because my dad said I can't just 'do nothing' after school." "The point is" shows how she has learned the habit to skip over sadness because she feels pressure to "quickly choose" the next activity in order to rescue her parents' affirmation and perhaps restore her parents' pride. Her parents do not take time to grieve, so why should she know how to grieve herself?

Adolescents grieve over their daily struggles, and the weight of this sadness and shame does not go away if ignored or denied. As one gifted piano-playing junior told me after he made a few mistakes in an otherwise amazing performance at a school event, "It's not *what* you do, but *how* you do . . . and today I screwed up." He left the auditorium burdened by the three or four missed notes and unable to rejoice in the thousands of beautifully played sounds. He paced around the emptying auditorium pulling up his collar to his ears and running his hands through his hair repeatedly, as if his head was going to explode with all the frustration and embarrassment inside it. I knew by his sunken shoulders as he quickly walked away that he would probably not volunteer to play for his peers again. Joining up with friends, I heard him start up a conversation by swearing loudly about the weather and teasing a girl for her hair. If he could have just stood still for a few seconds in the presence of adults, he would have heard all the affirming and celebratory words he needed from others. But he learned from somewhere or from someone that imperfections are shameful to grown-ups and that they eclipse any achievement. A sense of failure caused him, literally, to run away into the next moment or experience. What he clearly did not learn along the way was the ability to talk—without shame—through his own perception of performing, and to integrate into his assessments of himself the balancing love and affirmation of others.

The all-too-common teenage perception of the world as cold or unfeeling is strengthened when adults only talk about the events and outcomes of their lives, rather than the emotional experience of being alive. When adults avoid emotions, students learn to do the same. One obvious reason peer groups or romantic experiences are so powerful for teens is that such harbors of intimacy carve out a safe space for the endless talking and processing of feelings and reactions to the world that both grief and joy require. Adults who focus on looking forward or looking back on events for lessons learned or outcomes to avoid lose any chance to be the potentially helpful and hopeful voice of maturity. As one senior girl expressed it to me:

> I have so much to say to my mom, but we never really talk about feelings, so at this point, I don't know where to start. There's just too much that didn't get said along the way, and now there's just too much to cover, you know? But whatever... it's fine... I just save it or try to forget it... which is probably better because I don't have energy for her drama.

While adults want to hear what is or is not happening *for* teens, most teens want to talk about what is happening *to* them. Adult advice is powerful and necessary, but it is, in the end, *our* narrative and not theirs. Adolescents only trust listeners (of any age) who demonstrate real curiosity and admit that they need lots of information in order to understand. Teens tell me that they are willing to pour their hearts out to adults who earn the right to share their own adult perceptions and lessons—but only after extensive and nonjudgmental listening has been demonstrated. As one junior girl said about conversations with parents:

My dad busts in on conversations with me and my friends or my sister. He stalks our conversations from another room until he's had enough of all the words and then just walks in and shoots me with these random commands. I hate it. And he's like never actually right about what we were talking about. You can't just show up in a conversation at the end. Whatever. We just blow him off.

The result of young people perceiving and experiencing the world around them without much help from parents (beyond knee-jerk criticism or success-driven coaching) is that many adolescents are left alone or with their friends to form a moral and spiritual understanding of the world and of themselves. This process of constructing a face to show the world disappears further and further underground as our culture shows itself to be less and less accepting of uncertainty, imperfection, or disability. As a result, teens feel a need to put on a mask for their parents, their teachers, their coaches, and even their peers to hide all the mysterious or imperfect aspects of their being that require more parental loving than parental lauding. In the echo chambers of self and peer groups, our teens are trying to find meaning for their lives and choose worthy purposes for their gifts and passions. They are looking for safe spaces to say "I am not sure what I feel," or "I am not sure what I want." When adolescents look in the mirror, what kind of person have they become by the end of the high school journey? Are they proud of that person or uncertain? Are they ashamed of what they see? When our children leave us for college or other forms of independent life, it is essential to take stock of what their inner voice is whispering and how those thoughts might guide them or destroy them in our absence. When we read the self-descriptions of adolescents, we can learn what person our parenting and teaching has called forth.

What kind of armor can protect the adolescent against the pain of the world he or she sees? It can take many forms: deception, addiction, overachievement, underachievement, anger, bullying, violence, detachment, rebellion, starvation, cutting, or other expressions of depression or grief. Many families and schools are so success-driven that they sideline emotional and spiritual reflection time for and with teenagers, leaving them to hide their grief and fears in pursuits and habits that actually further undermine inner peace and mental health. So when adolescents lose at games or fail at other goals, they cannot help but feel shame in front of the adults who have failed to teach them to value failure and the lessons it teaches. We raise children who are learning to say, "I like eliminating my competition." Furthermore, negative habits such as lying or cheating that developed first as simple reactions to a competitive world are left hidden or ignored in those dark places where teens are all too aware of their presence and power. Teenagers look in the mirror and see a person who is being lauded by the world but one whom they do not always trust and of whose habits they are often ashamed:

> *I gossip.*
> *I have little self-confidence.*
> *I have a pretty bad and quick temper.*
> *I can be too self-centered.*
> *I am a really good liar because no one expects it of me.*
> *I have mastered lying and cheating. I hate it, but it's my*
>   *instinct at this point.*

Adding to this confusion over ethics is another trend in the talk of parents about values that I hear too often in post-game or post-performance conversations in the parking lots of fields or auditoriums. There is a clear premium placed on winning, but alongside that priority is the constant lifting up of virtue language—"Don't cheat, be a good friend, be generous"—despite the difficulty of reconciling these often competing values. The result is a child who knows that winning is still the main point but at the same time fears the shame for using short cuts, cheating, or other means to reach that goal. It is a classic double-bind: when parents present both winning and virtuous competing as *equal* goals, the child is left without the skills to choose one over the other when they conflict. And when the child senses that winning is more celebrated than virtuous winning or virtuous losing, it is obvious the path that he or she will take in the search for love and affirmation. As a coach of many sports at many age levels, I can say that few parents go out for pizza or ice cream to celebrate self-less playing as an end in itself, nor do most youth athletic leagues or performance clubs offer trophies to the losers for selflessness or moral heroism. The moral life becomes a series of choices between hard work and short cuts, and the reason many of my high school students describe the adult world with the phrase "the end justifies the means" is that they have had a decade of pizza to celebrate the end and not the means.

The result of the confusion created in children by hallowing moral heroism but affirming winners more than anything is that children begin to internalize the disconnect and learn to live with it. Adolescents learn to look virtuous while they strive for success at all costs:

> *I'm very competitive.*
> *I lie.*
> *What I do is never enough for myself.*
> *I always have to be right.*
> *I can be compassionate but I am equally capable of being*
>   *inconsiderate.*
> *I'm materialistic.*
> *I'm gay and tired of hiding.*

These habits of the divided person are what teenagers see in themselves and often they feel powerless and unable to change. I am often moved by how honest students can be about their moral confusions and their sense of shame for the tricks they have learned in order to be loved or valued, but looking in the mirror is difficult for them; their survival skills are not always ones they admire.

> *I mask my unhappiness to be comfortable with who I am.*
> *I need to be around friends to be happy.*
> *If there were really a Santa, I'd get coal.*
> *I don't show people how I am really feeling.*

Many teens also have a difficult time feeling proud of their own achievements, taking refuge in self-criticism, sarcasm, doubt, and detachment.

Augustine's *Confessions,* a young man's autobiography written seventeen centuries ago, contains this description of his adolescent years: "I had become a problem to myself.... What was it that delighted me but only to love and be loved?" What is even more relevant to modern-day teens is Augustine's observation that his parents were not helpful in raising him according to moral or spiritual expectations:

> *Nor were my parents concerned to cut short my downfall....*
> *Rather, they were wholly concerned with my learning to make*
> *as good a speech as possible and to be persuasive in the use of*
> *words.*

Augustine was morally and spiritually lost and broken as an adolescent, yet his parents were consumed by their concern over his progress in schooling and in the promise of a lucrative future in the professional world for their intelligent son. His confessions of the pains and problems of being a teenager echo in the popular lyrics, the images in tattoos, the T-shirt slogans, and the online diaries of countless contemporary teens. It is nothing new for teens to feel fiery passions alongside haunting emptiness. And it is not new for parents to worry more about whether or not their child will get a good job than whether or not he or she has the emotional and spiritual skills to know what jobs are worth doing.

To stand among teenagers in a classroom, in a locker room, or in a practice room is like looking in the lost-and-found basket in any airport or train station. Each one is known by someone, loved to some degree, and absolutely real. Yet most lost-and-found items are never claimed in our culture, mostly because owners do not know where to look. It is clear from the student quotations in this chapter that adolescents feel lost in the gap between what adults say we care about and how we live; these are children whose only safe family of relationships are the friends gathered more for survival than out of spontaneous connections: "I love my friends more than they will ever know. They are my true home." Many teens think and behave like aliens in the world and to themselves:

> *I don't feel at home anywhere.*
> *I have very little idea where I am going in life.*

I don't know if I actually want to go to college.
Sometimes I don't even trust myself.
I'm friends with people I don't like.
I am not truly happy, I don't know how to change it, but I
haven't been happy for a while.

Their words speak with little confidence that reconnections in relationships with parents, teachers, and even the environment are possible once they become teens: "I wish I could go back to the innocence of childhood."

Chapter Four

GOD'S AUTOGRAPH

Teenagers Talking about the Soul

*"Whenever my family is all home, and the floorboards
are creaking and alive, and my mom is yelling at
my brother, I know that my family has a soul."*

Needing a place to sit down with my heavy folders to do some work, I walked by a spare conference room in the school and saw an open space to sit at a long mahogany table. There was no one else except for one student working away on makeup assignments after an absence, who had also found the shelter of silence in an otherwise unmanageably loud high school world. "May I sit here and work?" Justin seemed flattered that I asked. "Yeah. And I can leave, you know." I dropped into the seat—"I'd love it if you stayed. Total silence makes me nervous." He looked delighted. "Me too!" We put our heads down and went to work.

I had taught this twelfth-grader more than once over his high school career and my respect for him had grown every year. He did not speak very often so I was not the only person who needed years to get a sense of him. Justin was a hard worker with an indomitable positive outlook. Two tireless parents, with the support of a large and involved extended family, raised Justin. His parents, aunts, and uncles were all refugees from Liberia. Even as a young person with much maturing to do, Justin always appeared grateful for the kinds of blessings often unnoticed by many middle-class teens, like a safe school or a good friend. More than one adult described him to me over the years with a phrase about the soul that is common in our culture: "That Justin is a good kid. He's got an old soul."

After a few minutes Justin asked what I was doing at my end of the long table, and I told him I was organizing student surveys. He seemed fascinated. "What questions do you ask? What's your favorite question to ask students?"

"Wow. That's a good question." He remained still, smiling and waiting for an answer. "Well, I love asking students to give me a definition of the soul." He digested each of my words. "Oh. Man. That's hard!" Then he picked up his pen with purpose. "You want mine?" I nodded. "Okay. I'll give you mine." He stalled. He put the pen down and rubbed his freshly shaven head with both hands. "Okay, give me some time, okay? You can go ahead and go back to your stuff. I'll let you know when I've got it." I went back to making piles to look busy and give him time to think.

After a few minutes, he declared, "I'm ready." I stopped everything. "Do you want a piece of paper?" He waved me off. "No. It's real simple." Almost with a wink, he added, "You'll remember it." He took a deep breath. "It's God's autograph." Then his face became serious, instructive. "You know what I mean, right? You ever seen one of those autograph books? Because people need somewhere to keep the real thing. That's what the soul is. It's God's *real thing*." He tapped his index finger on the table for each word of the sentence. "The real autograph of God...not a fake one. The *real thing*. That's what I got written in me." Justin tended his life with a strong sense of stewardship that adults could see but perhaps did not understand. His definition of the soul gave me a glimpse of what "real thing" he is taking such good care of every day.

I began teaching as an advanced placement history teacher, never wondering how or why my students used the word "soul" as often or as powerfully as they do. It took teenagers to prove to me the value and vital life of this word in their lives. Listen closely in our culture and you will discover that it is impossible to listen to music of any genre, to look at graffiti in any city, to read tattoos on any teen's body, or to keep track of the marketing language for products and services to teens and not see the word "soul." If you do not see it or hear it, you are looking in the wrong places in teen lives for their truths. I have grown into the conviction that when I do not read the word "soul" or hear it in music or other teen-consuming media, I am not listening hard enough or putting myself in the presence of teen lives. Hearing the word "soul" is the sign that you have arrived at the core of the hobbies and habits of teen hearts. They know the word "soul." They use the word "soul." In every color of pencil, pen, and marker scribbled by teens for a decade—from Boston to Salt Lake City to San Francisco—I have collected definitions and discussions of the soul bursting off page and after page in every box of my surveys and studies. These words about the soul are what hold and heal my hope for the future of our teens. Adolescents may hate the world and the person that this world is forming them to be, but they still believe in the soul. And they still love the soul.

When I read definitions of the soul written by my students each year, I am struck by the uniqueness with which each young person searches and struggles with words to express their spiritual truths. The definitions are so full of life and truth that when I read these curious, cryptic, colorful, and comical definitions, I can almost hear each student's actual voice, intonation, pauses, and emphases. From our time spent in the classroom together or my time spent conducting interviews, I can reconstruct an image of their gestures, smiles, and posture from words written years ago. Rarely does a written definition give me an impression of the student that I have not gathered, at least in part, from his or her presence. Though this connection between the mere words and the flesh-

and-bones of teens who speak them is hard to document, I am convinced that a teenager's soul definition tells us so much about her mental, physical, and psychological health. This definition is a priceless picture of who the teenager really is. Quite frankly, the written definitions not only *sound like* the students who write them, they very often *look like* the students who write them. Disheveled students write messy sentences. Obsessive-compulsive students write perfectly straight words and sentences on paper without preprinted lines. Shy students produce writing barely legible because they press so gently on the page. Extroverted girls write in bright, thick marker. Shy boys write in pencil. Anxiety-ridden students erase endlessly. Children of divorce ask constantly if what they have written pleases me, while children of alcoholics never seem to believe me that the amount they have written is enough for me.

Many times a written definition of the soul does even more— it has a way of clarifying or crystallizing to me something about the student's *persona* that I had never fully pieced together before I asked, "How do you define the soul?" The words used will very often provide a helpful and even unique way of correcting or clarifying my perception of who the teenager is and what he or she believes.

In adolescent writing about the soul, I find little to none of the posturing that is common when teenagers are asked to define themselves in non-spiritual terms. Too often adolescents slip into the flat language of cliques or anti-cliques, such as "jock," "geek," or "freak." In my experience, students usually define a "self" (theirs or someone else's) as part of a group or as decidedly apart from groups. But when defining the soul, students do not speak in categories or labels taken from adolescent social taxonomy. Most students appear unclear as to whether or not the soul is a "thing" or "substance," but they are sure that the soul is, in their word, "real."

Adolescents attach widely varying descriptions, purposes, and responsibilities to the human soul. The lack of desire or inability to define the soul as a bodily or physical entity frees the adolescent to speak of the soul as embodying or channeling realities beyond the material or medical. You can tell by the often explosive creativity in soul definitions that teenagers love this vacation from thinking of themselves only in the conventional categories of size, appearance, popularity, race, gender, or social status.

When I read the definitions from my own students and add them to those I have gathered from traveling to other schools and communities each year, clear trends emerge in the words, themes, images, and metaphors. The cultural references change: the hit music lyrics mentioned or the television sitcom characters footnoted for thoughts about the soul change every year, if not every month. But at the same time there are certain striking similarities.

First, adolescents seem to handle the ambiguity in describing the soul by thinking and writing in terms of *roles* rather than trying to describe the soul's being or essence. In short, they seem more comfortable talking about what the soul *does* than what it *is*.

Second, not a single student mentions the soul when defining the self or the world. It is abundantly clear that they are afraid of leaving high school, they are not always proud of the habits that got them through high school, they are uncertain of their gifts, and they tend to see the world as shallow, competitive, painful, bigoted, and selfish. But the soul itself does not enter into their immediate assessment of self or world. In my experience, a conception of the soul is a buried treasure.

Third, few students use the word "my" when defining the soul. Adolescents who revel in owning things in the way they speak— *my* friends, *my* music, *my* room—seem unable to speak of the soul as anything that they possess with confidence. This striking omission of ownership language for the soul helps to explain why the moral and spiritual powers of the soul fail to inform the daily decisions of my students. They believe in the soul in the way they believe they have a liver or a heart: yes, teens know these organs exist and they have learned their purposes over time. However, few seem to know (or care) how to cultivate the wisdom of the soul or follow its guidance.

We might think that students raised within a formal religion would have more to say about a spiritual idea such as the soul. However, I have found little difference in the intensity or creativity of soul definitions between students whose families practice a religion and those whose families do not. I have also found no statistically significant difference in soul definitions among students who practice different religions—the words of evangelical Protestant, Roman Catholic, or Jewish students rarely reflect the real differences among these faiths. In fact, most self-identified "religious" students state their belief that most religions share a similar definition of the soul, despite the fact that this notion is not borne out across traditions.

In fact, the students I talk to state that the word "soul" is not, for this generation of young people, a religious word at all. Among those students who attend or even love their church, synagogue, or mosque, I do not hear definitions of the soul that reflect much or any formal training on the topic. It may be that marketing and advertising departments speak of the soul with more passion and creativity than preachers do; the former have clearly picked up on the secret that young people love to think and speak about the soul and its needs. You cannot go a week watching television or the Internet and not be told that a particular product will touch, inspire, entertain, or even heal the soul. Can you say the same thing about your local religious organization?

In this section you will find a wide range of language about the soul coming from teenagers around the country, sorted into broad categories that I call "roles for the soul." My choice of these categories is itself a form of commentary on what I think some of this language means. You will notice that many definitions include multiples roles for the soul, but I contend that the general roles are nonetheless consistent across a wide spectrum. The spiritual wisdom and creativity of these students is humbling, and I hope this experience will bring you into some of the eclectic and dynamic conversations to be had with teenagers about the soul. Consider it a road map for your own reading and listening to the voices of adolescents.

1. *The soul sustains life.* Listen for the ways that the soul holds together and makes whole an adolescent's ideas, experiences, memories, and hopes for the future.

> *"It's like Pandora's box. It's hard to find but once you find it and open it, anything could be inside."*

The shifting plates of social life for the teenager leave even the most resilient and mature adolescents feeling lost, rudderless, and unstable while in high school. However, I do not believe adolescents suffer from feelings of being lost only because they have begun to separate emotionally from adults (differentiation) or away from their childhood sense of self (identity formation). As I have listened to teenagers narrate their own emotional and relational development, it seems that their nomadic sense of self is as much a result of adult influence as it is a reality of adolescent development. At a developmental stage when most adolescents are able to think more about others, to take on new perspectives, and to reach out to form bonds of friendship and loyalty, they are simultaneously asked by adults in our culture to do the reverse: to act independently from their friends, to compete ferociously with others in scholarship, sports, and performances, and to distinguish themselves apart from the pack. Adolescents seek connection; adults reward competition. They seek a vocation, or a calling; adults reward professionalism. They seek experimentation; adults reward expertise. It is no wonder that students feel isolated from adults, unsure of the direction for their lives.

And yet their definitions of the soul reveal a teenager's confidence that the soul is a stable foundation and a sustaining source of definition. Amid the shifting sands of their social landscape, the soul is a permanent, calm, and steady support system that grounds being, roots the self, and defines and defends the humanity of each person.

> *Soul is a person's inner being behind the exterior physical body that is who you truly are. It controls all your*

indefinable aspects or characteristics. It is the question why or what. It is like the cream inside cannoli, but it's never the same as the cannoli before. It is unique and new for each person. It is <u>YOU.</u> Not what you look like OR what your body is shaped like. (male)

For most girls, the soul establishes beauty and worth that is not based in physical appearance. However, the above definition was written by an athletic boy who also believes that the soul establishes beauty from within the person. The following girls echo this notion that the soul offers stability and worth because it holds and hides truths that the world cannot always see and rarely can appreciate.

I have no idea what a soul is exactly.
I think it really defines a person.
I associate it with positive things.
It's the person within the person—the body is like the "artificial" person because it's just what you see on the outside. (female)

It's the part of you that goes to heaven or hell when you die I think. It's shaped by your mind and who you choose to be, so it becomes the essence of who you are, sort of like you in your purest form. I think it is basically good in everybody, unless you do terrible things and irreversibly distort it, and it either becomes trapped in hell or free in heaven. . . . I think. I also don't think it can be completely understood because it's not meant to be. (female)

Girls and boys trust the soul even though they are not sure they know what it is. Both of these boys credit the soul with supplying and sustaining one's identity:

I have no idea, but it is something that everyone has. It is something that belongs completely to you and no one else. A soul gives you your identity, and helps guide you on what to do. (male)

Sort of like the essence of you, usually seen as a positive
good thing. It's something inherently human. The thing
that continues on after the body is gone (not attached to
earthly body).
If you didn't have one you wouldn't feel things like everyone
else. You would be inhuman, uncompassionate, etc.
If you sell your soul that's just seen as really low, you are
owned by whoever/whatever you sold it to.
Selling your soul to something is like being far too dedicated
to the something at the expense of your humanity.
Your soul is the only thing you have that can never be taken
away from you, if you sell it, it's like you don't value it.
(male)

Both girls and boys speak of the soul as being the "essence" of
a person, the true person beneath the physical body and the *per-*
sona that the world sees and judges.

It's the essence of what you love, what you believe in, and
who you are. It defines you. It controls you and it is you.
(female)

I see soul as something that can't really be proven or
explained. It's the essence of who a person really is that can
only really be found through truly knowing someone. The
soul is essentially the life of someone, it is who they are.
(male)

A soul is what makes a person unique in their personality,
thoughts, beliefs. Makes a person's actions unique. (male)

Some teenagers assign to the soul the role of sustaining functions of mind, such as memory, feeling, and intuition.

Part of you that some people can relate to and some people
can't.
How much you love someone usually means you are closer
to knowing their soul.
Eyes = "window to your soul"

Soul = your being, your representation after you die and what people remember of you (your memory is your soul)
The memory may involve your physical body, but your soul can also define you. (female)

Your soul is NOT an object of faith. Your soul is the combination of everything in and around you that defines who you are. Your soul is your experiences, your memories, your thoughts and your eyes. It consists of everything and everyone that you've touched and that's touched you. Your soul is everything that is you, everything that was not before you and what will not be after you're gone. (male)

Soul is the moral/spiritual/personal part of you. The soul must be a part of the mind because you understand it as part of your identity beyond the body. I don't even know how to define it. It's indefinable. The soul is what defines a person as an individual. (female)

Soul is like spirit. It's all about feelings/emotions. It's something inside of you. Soul gives you love, hate, individuality. Everyone has a soul but no one's is the same. (male)

Soul: a soul is the internal being of a person
What they truly think
All the things that make up a person's personality (male)

Your soul is what is inside of you
Your spirit
Who you are as a person in the inside
Your soul has no body—you can't see it—not tangible.
Your soul is like your intuition.
Your soul defines who you are as a person. (female)

I think soul is the most personal part of a person, it's a combination of everything that makes you a person—emotions, beliefs, feelings. Soul is really what makes a person who they are. It's not something that you can see. (female)

The soul is like the song "merry happy." It's not like it's a really happy thing, but the reason I care so much about finding the exactly right song, and the reason I love music so much, not playing it, just grooving out to it and being me, is because of my soul. When I listen to music I come up with new outfits, think of stories that appear to me. It is my soul. (female)

I think soul is something within every person that transcends your physical and emotional being. The soul is the heart of something and is personally defined by each individual. The soul is like the nature around us. It can be used for anything but should be respected and taken care of. It will then consequentially give back to its surroundings. (female)

To me a soul is everything the body is made up of, that does not have a shape or form. So basically, it's your personality, your conscience, your instincts, and your thoughts, all bottled up, that truly define you. (male)

*Every human characteristic that's not physical (i.e., not arms, legs, eyes, nose, etc.)
The soul is basically everything else
Personality, likes and dislikes, skills and talents
It is what defines us because it is what makes us different from other people. (male)*

Many students cannot name all the thoughts and emotions within them, but many young people state that the soul is where all these truths are kept. In other words, they may be unsure of *what* they feel, but they are sure *where* they feel it.

*It is the inner definition of one's self. It is who you are.
It's like Pandora's box. It's hard to find but once you find it and open it, anything could be inside. But once it is discovered, it is known only to you until someone else opens it. (male)*

Soul is your individual self and body. It is the essence of your being that is not seen by anyone throughout your entire life. Your soul shows your individual personality but it is deep in your being so people can't really see it. Like people who played blues used their soul while playing digging deep in your body to show your inner self. (male)

———————

2. *The soul acts from inside.* Listen for the ways that the soul energizes and impels the adolescent toward positive and heroic actions.

> *"A soul lets you truly live past the point of breathing and walking."*

Far from just an idea, the soul is also an active force within people that motivates them toward or away from certain actions and choices. Teens report actually feeling the soul pushing and pulling. The soul also speaks, guides, and comforts. It is an engine of meaning, purpose, and passion. According to the students in this section, the soul draws and pulls them into and through hard relationships and periods of suffering. It drives the person toward the good, and feeds on the good that someone does. Our souls are either made well or weak by the way we live.

A soul lets you feel empathy for the events in your life and the people around you. (female)

A soul is what makes us live.
Everyone has a soul and all are different.
People's souls are seen through their actions and character and personality. (female)

It is the part of you that is most connected to the earth and everything.
You can feel it in you.
A soul lets you truly live past the point of breathing and walking.
It's like a Sacher torte—it looks like an ordinary chocolate cake, but inside there is this sauce thing that's amazing

*and unlike anything I have ever tasted. I couldn't tell
you exactly what it is but it's the most mysterious
delicious thing ever!*
It's what connects you to others.
*You can feel it in certain moments—I feel it when I hear
music.*
*You can never lose your soul, you can forget about it for a
while, but it's still ALWAYS there.*
It's a part of your identity.
Yes it would matter if you didn't know about your soul....
You'd be incomplete, with one, life feels different. (female)

*Everyone has a soul. Our soul is one of many things that
define who we are. Everyone's soul is different and comes in
all shapes, sizes, and even color. Our souls, however, are not
visible to the naked eye. It is in acts, decisions, and choices
we make that show our true soul within. I believe a person's
soul is one of the most important aspects of a person.
Without a soul, we are not human.* (female)

*I have some idea. I think it's an invisible ball of gas that
lights up when it talks to you. I think a soul is something
different to everyone, and yet everyone has experienced its
existence at some point. A soul is what motivates and
inspired you to do whatever it was you needed motivation
of inspiration to do. I think it's broken down like this:*
  Soul = conscience, i.e. Jiminy Cricket
      +
  ambition, motivation, determination: all the -ations
      +
  the thing that makes you recognize your soul
      +
  love or whatever the thing is that allows you to love.
  (male)

*I'm not really sure if it's tangible energy coursing through
people or someone's personality in a deeper sense of the
word, like the thing about someone that's affected by the
world and reacts. Sometimes it seems like you can feel your
soul, it's a weird feeling that's probably based on hormones*

or other chemicals getting released for some reason, so it kind of feels like something inside your chest needs to get out but is tightening but it isn't a physical thing, and doesn't happen very often but it's definitely noticeable when it does. It feels like the limits of your emotional capacity, but it doesn't happen at particularly important moments. Yeah, I guess a soul seems like something distinct about a person and how they take things in and react.

I can't figure out if it's tangible or not, like a single entity, or the effect of energy atoms coursing through a brain, or if energy is made up of atoms at all, or maybe it's like God, it would mean anything (a creator, in physical form, the relationships and consciousness that strings together all mankind, or nonexistent) that's tough, it's something we'll never find out for sure, either. (female)

The purpose of a soul is to comfort people when they are faced with the concept of death. (male)

Soul is what comes from the heart, what you love, enjoy, and makes you truly happy. Everyone has one and knows what it is. Every single person has a different view on it. Without a soul life would be terribly different because there would be no passion. (male)

The soul is like oxygen, without it we would not be alive, but we don't know exactly why we need it. Scientists don't know why we need oxygen to survive as opposed to the more abundant nitrogen. We may have our theories about its purpose, but no concrete reason. What do they do? They give life. Without the soul there would be no humans. (male)

A soul is for living. It makes life more than beating heart, pounding blood, electrical signals, etc. It brings meaning. (female)

Soul is something that can be seen through someone's actions or words especially when someone is passionate about something.

*A soul is needed to imbue something with meaning and
  purpose. It is the core of humans including all our
  questions, fears and hopes. (female)*

*Everything about a person's personality stems from their
  soul.*
*The soul guides a person through life, helping them make
  choices.*
*Knowing yourself, or in essence knowing your soul helps a
  person live their life. (female)*

A soul can guide a person through life.
*A soul is your gut feeling, it tells you deep down your true
  feelings*
*A soul is supposed to lead you in the right direction (like
  deciding what to do) if you listen to it. I believe
  everyone's soul tries to guide you to truth. (female)*

Soul: the central force that leads someone on. (male)

*"Soul" is something that is hard for me to grasp and
  understand the meaning.*
*I think the soul is where we get the strong feelings form that
  take over like love, passion, honesty, and hope. These
  feelings are complicated and are found in our soul.
  (female)*

*Your soul is the being, personality, and beliefs that are
inside you that guide you to make decisions, love and
believe in God to name a few. (female)*

3. *The soul teaches moral lessons.* Listen for the way that students learn right and wrong from the moral voice of the soul.

> *"I believe my soul to be a second body for me, and therefore,*
> *I must take care of it by making the right decisions."*

A large number of adolescents in my research describe the world as broken, materialistic, unfair, racist, and deceitful. It is stunning to read such moral indictments of the culture from teenagers who nonetheless appear to enjoy trafficking in half-truths and treasure the techno-toys of our times. Like many adults, they both love and judge the world. Teens openly admit that they are also addicted to "the world," but they also state again and again—girls and boys—that they know addiction to "the world's shallow values" is hurting their souls. They discern mixed messages about meaning and morality from adults. They state openly that celebrity culture is pathetic; they wish desperately that the world did not "revolve around money." Teens hate injustice, racism, and war. Yet it is clear that the moral resource feeding their sense that things are not right or fair in "the world" is not religion or politics, but instead the moral voice of the soul.

> *The soul is kind of like your conscience. It's an inner spirit*
> *that determines right from wrong.*
> *"You can't sell your soul, it doesn't belong to you in the first*
> *place. It belongs to God."—from the 2006 movie*
> *"Bedazzled"* (male)

> *The soul always knows what is right vs. wrong.*
> *Body doesn't always listen to it.*
> *A soul lets someone show their true character.*
> *It's what makes someone stand out in a crowd.*
> *A part of me wants to believe that your soul can never die,*
> *it is only the body that carries it around that can be lost.*
> (female)

I usually somewhat associate it with a conscience. But more that the soul feeds off one's conscience. The soul is something you can't see, but you can kind of feel it. It is something no one really knows how to control, but it's a feeling that you can get when doing something good or bad and your soul will feel good or bad. (female)

Soul is a concept that helps explain what guides our moral compass and is our spiritual being which lives on after our death. Also, it is the essence of something. If you consciously consider the possibility that you have a soul, then you may live your life differently because of the possibility that it may be judged after you have died. (male)

Soul is the spiritual body that only you can see and those whom you love can see. It is the part of your being that is permanent. Your body is only temporary in this life, however your soul is the part of you that contains all of your traits, virtues, and also your faults. The soul, to me, matters. However, depending on your own beliefs, the soul does not have to matter. If I didn't have a soul, my life would be completely different. I believe my soul to be a second body for me, and therefore, I must take care of it by making the right decisions. In a sense, my right decisions are food for the soul, but my bad decisions are detrimental to the soul. My life would be completely different because then I would not be responsible for two bodies, just one, a physical body that will one day die. (female)

The inner part of you that will never go away. Provides the good in us. Couldn't live without it because it is a necessary part of us that God made in everyone. (female)

The part of your personality that controls your emotions, i.e., guilt, happiness, sadness. . . . Basically makes you who you are and determines your actions (or should). It doesn't really change, but it can fade out or become bigger (more important). A lot like the human heart, you can only go so far or do so well without it. (male)

*Soul is a combination of someone's beliefs, feelings, and
  values.
It determines how you act and how you develop
  relationships with other people.* (male)

*Your values keeper... it represents your morals. It leads a
path for your life. It gives you direction and purpose. The
soul is like education, you can take from it as much as you
think you should. Nobody can force it into you, you have to
want it.* (male)

---

4. *The soul is the voice of the spirit.* Listen for the power of the
soul to suggest and guide a spiritual life for the adolescent.

> *"Your soul is like God on speed dial."*

Most adolescents identify themselves with some kind of religious
tradition, and speak in positive, albeit tepid terms about the religion in which they were brought up. Many believe that religion,
on the whole, does more damage than good in the world, but in
their personal lives the teens I talk to value and enjoy religious
places as "peaceful" and "beautiful," and find most "religious people" in their lives to be "friendly," "kind," and with "strong personal convictions." About one in five mentions God in their soul
definitions and defines the soul's primary purpose as connecting
the person to God. But this is a fragile theism that rarely makes
any statements about how someone might be led by her soul to
think about or relate to God. Most students know little or nothing about the finer points—or even the major pillars—of dogma
or doctrine in their religious traditions. They haphazardly use
terms of judgment, heaven, or hell, though there is little conviction behind these ideas. Many otherwise articulate students have
trouble when they try to connect the traditional theological terms
of their traditions with their creative, nonconformist confidence
that the soul is a timeless source of personal, spiritual power not
related to explicit religious practices. Students write little about

who God is, but they are certain that the creator of the soul is God. Many of the most spiritual definitions of the soul do not mention the word "God," but try listening closely to the words they use—such as "voice" or "sense"—that point toward the presence of someone or something "other" whispering within the soul of the adolescent.

> *To me the soul is what goes to the next world in place of your physical body. Also, I think that it's the inner being that you hear when you are thinking. It's that little voice you hear. Everyone has a soul, and its food is prayer. Prayer helps the soul develop. (female)*

> *A fundamental, inherent essence of a human that exists and cannot be taken away.*
> *The soul is a human expression of something we don't understand, but want to. It represents the human desire for connection to each other and the world around us beyond the physical realm. To some, God is the source of this connection, or is this connection. (male)*

> *A soul is your true self—all that you are, all that you keep hidden, all that you show the world. . . . It's your good side, your demons, your gray areas. You don't have to show the world what your soul is, but it's there. It's everything that is not physical in you. It's your heart and mind together, and that creates your true self. The soul is there to give you individuality, to give you morals, emotions, humanity. It is you defined. Often it can be your best friend, sometimes your worst enemy. It's all of your voices combined into a single, multifaceted, intangible yet very real thing, unique to each of us. For me it's internal dialogue—by thinking so much about myself, my beliefs, my morals, I can more clearly see my soul and understand it. My soul matters so much to me—it's what guides me, wrongly or rightly, it's everything I am, good and bad. It's what makes me me. I couldn't live without it. It brings me to new realizations, new ideas, new reasons to be happy. Without it I'd be a*

shell. Literally. I would have nothing worthwhile to offer to the world. (female)

The soul is something that contains our personality and remains after we die. It is the part of everyone that is unique. I can't think of a metaphor to describe it because I don't think there is anything else like it. (male)

A soul is the part of a person that only God can see. Everyone can and does put on a mask to themselves and the world around them, hiding at any one time many parts of who they are. It is how God connects with humans, as it is where conscience, love, purity, and all good things about human nature reside. If someone lived without a soul (and some people do), they would be Godless. They would continue to live on earth, but would not continue past death to live (it makes sense, I swear!). I tried to come up with a metaphor for the soul, but I can't because there's simply nothing else like it in the world. (female)

Define the soul? That's REALLY hard.
Soul is your personality (so, you without your body).
Spiritual aspect of you.
Soul is like. . . ? Something that people take for granted.
Used a lot as a word but no one really knows what it is.
That thing that you love. Maybe a tradition.
(It's you.)
That Simpson's episode when Bart sells his soul. (female)

It is something abstract. Your FAITH allows you to know it exists.
Goes to heaven with you.
EACH SOUL is unique—it tells your story—the hardships you faced, your sins.
Without a soul we would lose our connection with God.
Your soul is like God on speed dial. (female)

Soul is all parts of yourself that are not physical. It is your personality, responsible for how you act, it is your conscience.
Soul is formed by experiences and upbringing.

Your soul is what makes you you.
It defines you.
No good or bad souls since good and bad are relative, souls
*   are only unique.*
Sometimes religion and others try to mold your soul into
*   something it may or may not be.* (male)

I believe that the soul is the only part remaining after death.
For me it is best defined as who you are and what you do
when no one is looking. (male)

The ghost inside a human for going to heaven or hell or
purgatory. (male)

Soul—your innermost feeling and thoughts.
Your spiritual guide to get through the world's sin. (male)

A "soul" cannot be defined because it is too complex for
humans to comprehend. It is the only thing humans can do
nothing to explore, change or damage. A soul is eternal and
eternity will never be understood no matter how long
humans exist. (male)

innerness
inner eternal life that carries on after death
Just chills and gets blamed for person being good or bad!
*   (ex. when people say "a bad person is soulless").* (male)

Once your body dies, your soul goes up to Heaven.
Cannot give your soul to the Devil. (female)

Spirit, essence, what defines who you are spiritually, who
you are in relation to God, all the things that make you a
good/not so good person. You cannot sell your soul, even
though Bart Simpson did. I believe that without a soul, you
would lose your personality and ability to make your own
decisions. (male)

5. *The soul is a social force.* Listen for the ways that the soul connects the teenager to others and to the world.

> *"Without it we would constantly be stabbing each other in the back, the world would all be about surviving and reproducing, not caring about each other."*

Perhaps the most predictable role for the soul among teenagers is the social role. In accordance with their dawning developmental abilities, many adolescents credit the soul with bonding them to other people and to God. With every passing year, I have more and more students who extend this connection to the earth, seeing the planet as another potential friend. In any case, students credit the soul for being an internal outlet that allows others to plug in and form strong, meaningful relationships. Students speak often of the soul as the source of one's individuality, but at the same time they believe there is an aspect of the soul that is a shared reality in everyone that allows us to accept difference and establish connections with any and all human beings.

> *The soul is not only universal but it is individual. Everyone has a soul that binds us to one another spiritually but each person has their own unique soul. A soul is the tingling in your toes, the knots in your stomach, the voice in your head. It is part emotional, part spiritual, part intellectual. It is your entire personality. The essence of you. It is like a book: the cover is the exterior but the words are the soul. Without a soul, a person would be like a book without words, merely a cover with nothing inside. (female)*

> *The soul is how you interact with other people. It's just a reaction, the first thing that pops into your head when you are faced with different situations. When you see someone in trouble or feeling tough times . . . do you help them? To an extent, every person thinks and feels a little different and that feeling is their soul. No soul is better or worse than*

another. Souls can be changed by different impacts or it can stay the same, depending. (male)

Soul is one's inner self/spirit. The soul is there to differentiate between people and is the basis for all relationships. Without a soul or something driving someone to do what they do, we would not know who we want to be with. The soul is like our conscience, but with so many other qualities. (female)

The soul is what prevents humans from being animals. Without it we would constantly be stabbing each other in the back, the world would all be about surviving and reproducing, not caring about each other. In some cases you can see soulless people, who only work for themselves, but for the most part people care about other people. Going back to the first sentence, people are more intelligent than animals, but what makes us different is that we care about each other. We can work towards something greater than ourselves. It is both our intelligence and our compassion that separates us. (male)

Essence, individual, but we all have one and therefore we share something indefinable and intangible—it makes us different and the same. I think of it as a compass. Can't see or feel it but it's the most important part of us because it makes us unique. (female)

Soul is the spirit within someone that makes them who they are. If a group of people has a common interest, then their souls connect, hence "soul food."
A thing that defines a person but that is unexplainable. (female)

6. *The soul inspires metaphors.* Listen and enjoy the metaphors to describe itself that the soul inspires in the minds of young people.

"The body is the shell, the soul is the pearl."

Without question, the most inspiring words written about the soul are encountered in the metaphors that teenagers offer to describe the indescribable reality and experience of the soul within them. Every year, there is at least one student who describes the soul as a Twinkie—looking like a simple cake on the outside, but shocking and blessing its consumer with a pure and delectable unexpected essence hidden within. But relationships with teenagers have proven to me that metaphors are not just a means to describe the elusive human soul in language. There is more a sense that the soul enables the student—by his or her own admission—to conceive and to employ metaphors as a way of making meaning. The soul has the role of metaphor-maker. Listen to these students and you will hear that the soul is the heartbeat of the imagination, the pump that produces meaning.

> *Your soul is who you really are, your values, your beliefs, your humor.*
> *It belongs to you, your instinct.*
> *Like a candle—your soul shines through the outside wax.*
> *You can see people's souls when you talk to them and they're describing something they're passionate about.* (female)

> *I feel like there are types of souls. It's definitely a positive thing. Can be religious or not. Soul food/music is comforting. The soul is the good in people—natural goodness.*
> *It's like climbing into bed when you are really tired and you just snuggle up into your covers and are engulfed by comfort and warmth.*
> *It's what we feel and what we remember.*
> *It is ours.* (female)

A soul is a supernatural gene. It is a spirit that controls the traits of a person that DNA is not responsible for, such as decision-making and things that you like. (male)

A soul is who a person really is. It's like a cheese Quesadilla, it's the awesomeness inside you. Your soul takes you to heaven. Yes, the soul matters. I think I would have a different life if I didn't know about it. I would live differently if I didn't have a soul. (male)

There are two different ways of thinking about a soul: the Bill Paxton version of Casper in which the soul is a rotund, white, ethereal ghost or we can see the soul as a feeling. Whenever my family is all home and the floorboards are creaking and alive, and my mom is yelling at my brothers, I know that my family has a soul. The soul cannot subtract from the value of a life, it does not add either, consciousness of the soul only allows us to love deeper. (female)

The soul is like the valuables in a safe deposit box—it's not the outside that's important, but what makes up the inside. (female)

The soul is like a warm piece of bread and you have to bite into it to actually know the warmth.
Traumatic experiences or great experiences can transform the soul (female)

The soul is one's passion, compassion and genuine emotions. . . . Your soul is like the water that fills a pool, because without it you are essentially empty. You and others can sink or swim, but either way the water has a powerful influence. The water could be cold or warm but you don't know how it will affect you and others until you dive in and experience it. (female)

A part of oneself where there is a concentration of being. It is what can define an individual. Not a conscious part of the person, but an undertone. The soul is like the abstract beyond the conscious mind. (male)

Soul to me is something that is inside of someone but not physically. I don't believe that the soul can be defined in just words. The soul can be viewed in so many ways just like love can be defined in many ways. (female)

I think the soul is who they really are all together, not just what you see on the outside. It is like the message behind a funny TV show. The soul guides a person through life, leading them in general directions toward decisions. (male)

The "soul" is one's inner spirit. The soul gives meaning to life. It's like a compass—it kind of points you in the right direction, but not really. (female)

It is something inside of every person that gives them energy, love and fun. The soul is like looking at an average building but stepping inside and hearing beautiful and fun music with awesome food and a fun, enthusiastic atmosphere. When people look at someone they look normal but when they get to know them, they find they are so interesting and fun on the inside. (female)

It is like goggles underwater, without them it would be hard to see anything but with them you can see more distinctly and make your decisions accordingly. It is a guide. (male)

The belief or thought that there is a part of your being that is eternal. An idea is like the soul of a society. Ideas live on forever even after the person that thought of the idea is dead. In that manner, ideas are eternal. (male)

Immeasurable, not just confined to one's own body.
One soul is like a single puzzle piece that is a unique addition to the complete picture of universal consciousness too complicated to be sensed by the human senses (i.e., can't be seen, touched, heard, tasted).
Reminds us that there are things beyond the physical world that are just as crucial to life as internal organs. (female)

Soul is like the wind, you can't see it but you know it's there. Sometimes you can even feel it. (male)

The soul is like the instrumentals in a song. Because it is the type of instruments used and the type of notes played that defines what kind of song the song is. The same goes for the soul. It is the types of likes/dislikes etc., that define one person. (male)

The soul is a hug and a long talk. The soul is where you live and how you live.
A soul is for existing and it keeps you human.
You can be living, but the soul makes you a person/individual. (female)

It is comprised of their personality, humor, intelligence, quarks, likes, dislikes, interest, characteristics, ambitions, etc.
It is everything you can't see in a person.
A body is a shell, the soul is the pearl.
A shell is meaningless but it's what's inside that gives it its meaning the pearl. (female)

A defining experience or attitude
The inner essence of someone
Ray Lewis, an NFL football player, said he "hit people to take their souls."
Soul is like the seeds in an apple—once the apple is eaten or decayed, the seeds are left to grow something new.
One's soul is what lives after one's body is gone.
Part of one's soul lives in their friends and family when they die. (male)

These adolescent reflections on the soul give us a glimpse of the complexity and beauty of their inner lives. For these teenagers the soul is an active force, a moral voice, a social fabric, a religious re-source, and a workshop for making metaphor. But if we look only to their definitions of the soul, we might be lulled into thinking that these teenagers are already masters of the spiritual capacity they profess—a group of teens who are as peaceful, moral, spiritual, and inspired as their soul conceptions promise. But as we have already seen, teens are far from peaceful. Many describe themselves as immoral. They long for a stable place in the social order of high school so desperately that they lie, gossip, binge, and purge to attain it. They describe the soul as having powers to help them, if not set them free, in their daily struggles and endeavors. However, my students are not capable of taking these beliefs they profess and incorporating them into their daily lives. Their lives and their world are nowhere near as beautiful and positive as the landscape of their soul. My students seem unable to gain confidence or a sense of vision from their conceptions of the soul. In a word, they lack the spiritual skills to put their beliefs into practice.

That is why there is such a serious gap between how students define the soul and what they perceive about themselves and the world:

I talk about people behind their backs too much.
Money and jealousy can control people and change them
for the worse.
I have mastered lying and cheating. I hate it. It's my instinct
at this point.
What you do doesn't matter as long as you don't get caught.
Nice guys finish last, unless they know the right people.
I lie, even when there is no purpose. I like making other
people happy.
Sometimes I feel like my friends just don't understand, even
though I love them to death.
There's still a lot of discrimination even though we pretend
we've gotten so good. Looks matter more than
personality a lot of times. So many people just pretend
they care about important things.
I hate when people lie, I am forgiving, but lying is the
hardest thing for me to forgive especially when it is to
myself or to those close to me. I feel like I have very few

*true friends, maybe because I have my guard up in fear
of getting hurt.*

*The world is not fair. You have to have money to survive in
this cut-throat world.*

*For once in my life, I really want to be able to say exactly
what I feel inside. That's not my life though . . . most of
the time when I'm angry, I just don't speak, or I smile
and fake it.*

*Having lots of money when I get older is my number one
goal.*

*Honesty can sometimes screw you over, even if it's always
the right thing to do. Secrets don't stay secrets for very
long.*

*I am gay and getting tired of hiding. I protect everyone
around me, regardless of whether or not they deserve it. I
love who I am.*

We are uncomfortable with the people we really are.

*I expect to succeed without working too hard, which is bad.
I am a really good liar because people don't really expect
it of me.*

*The world sucks. I hate it, but I used to love it. It pays to
cheat. Love should be number one, but it isn't.*

I am scared about growing up and becoming an adult.

*To be successful you have to have money. To make money,
you have to lie and cheat. Race, gender, looks all dictate
how successful an individual can be.*

Notice how many of these students confess lying, cheating,
and being manipulative with peers or parents. Notice how many
express feelings of grief about getting older or losing their innocence, and the resulting feelings of being lost or uncertain about
the unfolding future. Teenagers find it difficult to trust themselves
and to trust others. They feel unprepared for the world they will
have to enter, certain that it is morally and environmentally sick.
These revelations of how they perceive themselves and the world
show us where specifically we need to help students apply their
convictions about spiritual capacity and hope. Students speak
hopefully, even lyrically, about the soul, but it is a tool they do

not know how to use to heal their inner brokenness and the social brokenness around them. Their parents, teachers, and mentors need to find ways to help them unlock the riches of the soul
that they already believe in. We do not have to convince teens that
inner resources for meaning and value exist; they already sense
such potential is within every person. What they lack are the skills
of the soul.

 *Chapter Five*

TOOLS
NOT TOYS

Skills for the Soul of the Adolescent

"I often wake up with a feeling of being afraid. Sometimes I understand why I am afraid, but sometimes I can't figure it out. It's like I am waiting for the thing I am afraid of to arrive and then it will make sense. When I couldn't figure it out as a kid, I told myself it was monsters. Now I don't know what to make up to make sense of it. But calling it 'the future' works pretty well so far."

What strangles the imagination of the adolescent and keeps them from developing the skills that free the soul for joy and hope is fear. To handle their fears, teenagers often ape the adults around them by putting energy and trust into the pursuit of material things and the career paths with salaries that allow for competitive consumption. Their hope in a "good life" is like a fragile wish made while blowing out candles at each new birthday. Many of the anxieties reported by adolescents are expressive of the fact that they feel unprepared to survive, much less thrive, financially, emotionally, or spiritually in the adult world.

Over my years of surveys and interviews, I have found a particular question that shines a light on the skills that teens are asking for. When I ask them to complete the sentence, "When I worry about my future, it is because...," the fears teens express point directly to the weak points in their set of life skills and spiritual skills. Adolescents feel afraid when they lack the skills to face fear-ful challenges. Here is a short sample of the most commonly of-fered answers students have given over the past decade when asked to name their fears for the future.

I worry I will not be a successful father/mother
I worry about changes
I worry that marriage doesn't last
The stress levels of others scare me
I am afraid because the world is being so messed up by
 people
I fear failure and it paralyzes me
I fear being alone
I fear not finding a spouse
I fear I will never have enough money
I am afraid that I won't keep promises
I fear not having the money to support a family
What if I end up alone?
I am afraid because the world is not safe
I am afraid of war
I fear social pressure to succeed economically
I fear the crazy expectations of grown-ups
I am afraid of my parents' judgment
I am worried about death
I'm afraid I can't keep up doing well when I am on my own
I fear messing everything up
I'm afraid to be on my own
I'm afraid I will fail and waste everyone's love

What is clear from this list is that our teenagers are afraid of fail-ure, are uncertain of their ability to meet expectations, and ques-tion their ability to maintain healthy and lasting relationships. The statistics of marriage and divorce in this country help to ex-plain the widespread worry among teens that they, too, will break promises, refuse to reconcile, refuse to forgive, or lose hope. As students whose lives have been highly controlled by the interventionist culture of parenting the college-bound child, teens are petrified of losing control of circumstances. Chaos is their enemy. Their stated fears about not being able to maintain relationships demonstrate that they know little about the ways to heal from breaches of trust, misunderstandings, or failure. Middle-class teenagers today have been mostly protected from chaos and therefore lack the confidence to confront it. Of course, illness and death that can visit adolescent experience cannot be controlled by even the most intensely interventionist parent, leaving students fearful of how they will ever deal with the finality and sadness of death.

Financial insecurities plague the vision of students of all economic classes. The word "money" is one of the most commonly used terms when students talk about their thoughts, hopes, or fears of the future. Teens who are poor fear perpetuating poverty or failing those who raised them with soaring hopes and expectations that the next generation will escape the trap of financial insecurity. Middle-class children have been raised to reach up the ladder at every turn in life, leaving them exhausted from being either the 24/7 motor of their own mobility or the disappointing player who could not keep up with the pack. And the affluent adolescent has the burden of copying adult accomplishments with almost no authentic opportunities to develop the skills of independence or self-reliance. I have never met a teenager of any social class who did not, at some deep level, fear money.

From these fears we can form a map of skills that we need to name and to nurture among teenagers. They need us to speak and show our skills in making and keeping promises. We have to be as public at home and in the media about successful marriages and families as we are about scandals and failures. We have to celebrate promises made and kept in our families as much as we celebrate trophies won. Adolescents need us to explain what it means to criticize constructively and to forgive as a path to peace. And most importantly, we need to model that failure is a part of life and learning, not always a malfunction of life or a sign of ignorance. It is not enough to say that promises are important or that failures are an opportunity to heal in ways that produce greater strength for the soul. Many adults speak like this every single day.

But when you listen to the stated fears of teenagers, it is clear that they are listening not to our words, but to our actions. They are measuring our marriages, noting the cruel criticisms we make of others, and copying our spending habits.

"Failure to thrive" is a medical syndrome that describes an abnormality in the process of development of a baby in the first few days, weeks, and months of life. Medical students are trained to diagnose it; parents are trained to dread it. When a baby is labeled FTT, it means that there are major organs, systems, or other processes of essential growth that are not taking place and can lead to the eventual disability or even death of the child. Doctors who work with geriatric patients use the same term for decreased vitality in the elderly—that is, the abilities and habits necessary for healthy life are frail, fading, or not present.

I wish we had a phrase like "failure to thrive" for teenagers in whom essential moral and spiritual growth is slowing or fading and threatening the vitality of life. Many students who possess a great many intellectual, artistic, and athletic gifts, from families of all social classes making heroic attempts at providing the resources for success, have tired, fearful, and uncertain souls. Their souls are failing to thrive. Over time, this spiritual frailty can become more and more pronounced, even as other kinds of academic or athletic achievements pile up. The uncertainty in their eyes can turn slowly into darkness, even while these same teenagers are taking harder and harder classes, earning good grades, and developing by the month ever more marketable skills. This can be the hardest problem to notice and address in a young person, especially if that young person has learned to impress adults. What's more, the teenage soul is wired to thrive. Therefore teenagers who cannot shake feelings of emptiness and darkness often turn on themselves in anger and punishment for failing to thrive inside, practicing the many forms of teenage self-abuse, such as addiction, self-injury, rebellion, dangerous sexual experimentation, or other high-risk attempts to feel alive somewhere inside.

"When I think of my future, I'm worried because I'm not sure
I can keep things going as good on my own. At this point,
I'm not sure if I am where I am because of me or my parents.
It's hard to know where they end and I begin."

What are the skills we need to teach our young people in order to best prepare them to face themselves and the world, but also to know, love, forgive, and heal themselves and the world? Those of you who frequent parenting websites and bookstores know all too well that curious adults do not suffer from a lack of lists about "essential skills for young people." Quite the opposite is true. There are too many articles, studies, sermons, DVDs, and books that list the "essential skills" young people—in some cases, all people—need for happiness and wholeness. Yet I have learned from listening to teenagers to appreciate the fact that each adolescent voice and the nexus of needs it represents is different. Each adolescent need often stems from a unique personal, psychological, familial, or social situation. Therefore each solution—if it is to be a lasting spiritual or psychological improvement—must have some unique connection to your particular adolescent. Someone's book, column, or website cannot always give you the relevant map to the soul of the adolescent standing in front of you or the teen who has just walked away from you.

In this section we will consider four specific skills for the adolescent soul. Although every teenager has his or her own story, full of unique personalities, pressures, and potential, I have found that these four skills aid nearly all teenagers in their journey to a healthy adulthood:

1. The practice of delaying gratification

2. The habit of empathy

3. A sense of "enough"

4. The ability to forgive.

Skill One:
DELAYING GRATIFICATION

> *"The answer to every question about*
> *when I need to own something is NOW."*

The prevalence of cheating in America is staggering. There is not an age group beyond preschool where cheating in some form is not a reality. Children cheat, teenagers cheat, spouses cheat, investors cheat, celebrities cheat, professional athletes cheat, politicians cheat. Any teenager will tell you that she or he "has been told" never to cheat. But she will also tell you that she has cheated. I have never met a student who thinks cheating is "right," but I have also never met a student who has not confessed to cheating at some point. If you ask teenagers whether or not a person should cheat, they say "of course not." If you ask them if cheating is an inseparable part of life in school and in adult life, three out of four will say "of course it is." If you ask teenagers if they "plan to cheat in school or adult life," they will say "of course not." If you ask them if they might wind up cheating at some point in adult life, three out of four will say "at some point, probably."

My observation of the cheating habits of teens convinces me that the cause of cheating is not a strategic attempt to get ahead or acquire the potential spoils of cheating. Instead, I see teens trying to manage their intense natural and parent-nurtured desire for success. But many lack the skill of delayed gratification, so when the desire to succeed is intense and the skill level to delay gratification of that desire is lacking, the most natural outcome is cheating. Most students will tell you on surveys that they "hate cheating" and "hate" the cheating they have done and that they see around them. Nevertheless, cheating is in the air we breathe because it resolves the anxious desire to succeed among those who lack the ability to work hard for success without short cuts. Cheating is a balm for the hurried and harried child. Cheating is a short-lived but powerful relief of the impossible pressure of wanting to win all the time. It is medication for a disease—the inability to wait, to suffer through trial, pain, failure, or delay in the development of a product or acquisition of a habit or talent.

Behavior modification has become a religion in the rearing of children in this country. Whenever I make a house call to one of my students or former students at times of family celebration or crisis, I take note of the use of space on the refrigerator, the corkboards, or the walls of the teenager's room. Medals, ribbons, and certificates rewarding everything from participation to mastery often outnumber any child-created drawings or casual photos. And where there are photos, they usually document moments of success, elation, or winning, not the documentary evidence of the hard, daily work of being a person or a team or a family. These photos are the two-dimensional trophies to accompany the three-dimensional trophies that mark an American home as inhabited by successful people.

The problem with trophies or college acceptances or job offers is that they do not always go to the person who has worked the hardest. Teenagers know this. And therefore many teens speak as highly of things like "luck," "connections," or "karma" as they do of habits like studying, practicing, and enduring failure. The fickle nature of "success" in our culture creates mythologies based on the idolatry of the lucky. Students will profess the tenants of this odd but ubiquitous mythology and argue that "being in the right place at the right time" or "knowing the right people" are the most important elements of success. Having the right skills, work ethic, or endurance is, in the words of one student of mine, "so old-school!" As one senior girl put it, "Success comes when someone picks you. And being picked is only partly about being good at something. It's mostly about being good at being picked."

A student of mine was looking at the new cell phone of his classmate. "Are you coveting your neighbor's goods?" I asked playfully. The small class shared a collective giggle. "I *want* that thing," the boy said without taking his eyes off the high-end cell phone of his peer. "I *must* have that thing." I tried to resolve the awkward moment. "Well, find out how much it is and then you can figure out when you can buy it." I said this more for the benefit of the classroom of students listening to the exchange than as a real suggestion for this particular student. I knew him well. He did not have a job and despite receiving an allowance from his family for (occasionally) doing some chores in the house, he had never had a job. He was very intelligent, but rarely met deadlines or gave attention to details of any kind, whether homework or hygiene. His current cell phone was only slightly less expensive than the one he was admiring. But he heard what I said and he took his eyes off the phone long enough to say calmly to me, "*When* I can own it?" He looked back at the phone with a longing smile. "The answer to every question about when I need to own something is NOW." For him, identifying the want *was* the accomplishment, not the impetus to work for it.

As long as we keep giving money to children who do not earn it or allowances to young people for infrequent completion of chores, we cannot be appalled by the choice to cheat when a challenge requires skills we have not taught. Instead of modeling delayed gratification—that is, showing our kids that we value practicing more than winning and principles more than outcomes—many parents practice *delayed affirmation*. This practice in an operant conditioning parenting style is based on the emotional manipulation of a person by showering rewards or withholding affirmation in order to condition the young person to seek outcomes pleasing to us. By delaying the forms of our excitement or affirmation—the pizza party, the favorite meal, the wrapped present—until a child has done or won something, we focus our love's manifestation on outcomes. Since affirmation is one of the main currencies of value for teenagers, they learn quickly in a trophy-centered world that love comes at the finish line, not the starting line. Cheating is the path too often taken not because it is the safest or even the fastest way to the finish line. Rather, by the parenting we practice, it might be the fastest way to feeling loved. Who can blame anyone for running toward that goal? Yet adolescents will develop skills of patience and work ethic, even in horrendously difficult circumstances, if they believe that they are loved in the process and in the moments of developing those skills. Spend time with teenagers and you will soon learn that they would sit in hell if they were loved there; likewise, they would rush out of heaven if they felt unloved there.

Skill Two:
THE HABIT OF EMPATHY

> *"I had a long conversation last night with a really good friend*
> *I have known for years. I learned something HUGE about him I*
> *never knew. Now I find myself wondering what else I don't know."*

Educators speak often about nurturing "empathy" in students. I
prefer to speak always of the "habit of empathy," in recognition
that empathy is a living, breathing state of mind that grows from
a set of principles and a set of practices. When I ask students to
define empathy, they usually describe a "mood" or a "feeling" they
have when they see a person going through a situation that is understandable or shared. Any teacher will tell you that there are
moments when certain students display a stunning and beautiful
sense of empathy. These moments inspire us as teachers or parents. We feel gratified that our efforts to raise or teach have proven
effective. But teachers and parents also have the frustrating experience of witnessing these very same students display reckless self-
ishness or carelessness for others. The student who eagerly and
joyfully came on the community service trip and served lunch or
played checkers with the homeless will not share his packed lunch
with a fellow student who forgot his own. The student who traveled to poverty-stricken Appalachia to build homes with Habitat
for Humanity tells a joke about "white trash" or "trailer trash"
poor people a week after he gets home. The student president of
the Black Student Association uses the "N" word around certain
friends. The poor white student on the Student Diversity Com-
mittee teases the Hispanic janitor after hours at school. The girl
who got cut from the musical teases the boy who got cut from the
basketball team.

One of the reasons that empathy is such an important skill for
teenagers is not simply because it rescues them from ignorance or
enhances their understanding of the personality or plights of others; it can also save them from self-destruction. When teenagers

can recognize some of themselves in others, this connection serves to heal their own soul's loneliness that too often becomes a void filled with distractions or destructive choices. In an overly competitive society where "every man is to another a wolf," teenagers are rescued by the idea that they are connected to other people by nature and not just by choice. A habit of empathy—that is, a constant focus on the universality of things like human dignity, inherent worth, potential, shared hope and fears—reminds a teenager that to be alive is to share life with others. This is what I tell my students when we speak of empathy: there are countless lives, but all lives share the experience of life. When they hear that "empathy" is simply what it feels like to remember that no one is ever alone in their experience of life, they want empathy every moment.

Of course, empathizing with others requires time. You cannot know that someone else is sharing your experience of life without talking, listening, or watching them live. The reason some of our young people can show bouts of empathy followed by bouts of callousness is that they believe empathy is a mood and they expect that moods will come and go. On surveys, students report that "empathy" is to them a reaction; most students will say it is the "best" reaction or a "loving" reaction, but it is a reaction in any case. Empathy, to many teenagers, is not a *cause* or *source* of feelings; rather, it is one of many feelings that they have when they witness another person's life situation, their joy or their pain. In other words, they do not begin the day feeling empathetic, but they might end it that way as they process the images and people of their day. With this understanding of reactionary empathy, the most we can hope for is a teenager who nurtures a habit of reacting to others with empathy. But this reaction, even if it becomes habitual, will not heal or even address the deepest needs of the adolescent soul for ongoing connection and community.

In order to draw out an *empathic life* from students, rather than merely reward or ritualize their *empathetic responses* in isolated situations, we need to remind and model to students the joy and healing of loneliness that comes from seeing the world through empathetic eyes. If a student asks you why you volunteer to feed the homeless, you can encourage empathetic living by saying, "I have met amazing people who are homeless. They have taught me things. They have made me laugh. They have shared their favorite foods and told some of the funniest jokes I have ever heard." These are all ways of holding up before the teenager the power of seeing ourselves in others. It shows teens that our adult lives become richer when we admit, share, and celebrate the fact that other people in very different lives share our hopes, dreams, skills, and fears. I cannot think of any high-risk behavior of a teenager that is a completely solitary endeavor. Even those addictions to negative thought patterns or to drugs or alcohol that exist in the shadows of a teenager's life are usually attempts to reach out for connections with others. The eating disorder aims to improve the body image for acceptance *from others*. The drug addiction continues to soothe the pain of disconnection or rejection *from others*. The cheating habit aims to receive praise *from others*. The over-exercising while no one is around is meant to protect against the bullying *from others*. Loneliness in the soul of the adolescent is a black hole that frightens and drives him or her toward any immediate fill. And the desire to be known and loved despite one's imperfections is one of the most powerful levers in the teenage soul. The habit of empathy is the skill to know and love another person as a fellow steward of a soul. When this skill emerges, I have seen young people freed from the tyranny of teenage loneliness. In giving the love they crave to someone whom they have come to see as craving the same love, they are renewed in hope that such love is possible and real, and that the desire to give it and receive it connects them at their core to other people. The reaction of empathy can change a teenager's mood; the habit of empathy can change or even save his life. The habit of empathy is the vaccination against loneliness, which is the most destructive force in the soul of teenagers.

Skill Three:
A SENSE OF ENOUGH

> *"What do you mean by 'enough'? I know what 'a lot'*
> *feels like. I know what 'nothing' feels like.*
> *But I don't know what 'enough' feels like."*

When once asked, "How much money is enough money?" the titan John D. Rockefeller famously answered, "Just a little bit more." I hear that kind of thinking from teenagers all over the country, in every social class. Even my most intelligent and mature students pause or stutter or shrug when asked these simple questions:

* "How much money would be enough money for you to be happy?"

* "How many rooms would be enough rooms for a house that you might want to own?"

* "How many days of vacation each year would be enough days for you?"

* "How many presents would be enough presents for your birthday?"

* "How much chocolate would be enough chocolate for your dessert?"

I rarely hear students use the word "enough." The only times you will hear it among young people is when they are measuring something they don't like. The word "enough" is their way of saying "Stop!" or "End!" When yelling at a friend who is being too critical, a teenager might yell, "I've heard enough from you!" It is a negative term, a word thrown at others to end a negative behavior. Its use among teens is to break off a conversation or a relationship rather than help or heal one. It is throwing a red flag, not waving a white one. Teens use it as a last defense, as a word that says someone has selfishly or destructively crossed a necessary boundary. It is a teenage way of saying "I give up," or even, "I quit."

Adolescents respond to questions about what they want, and are equally quick to tell you what they hate. But when you ask them to consider the word "enough" in a positive way—as a way to mark the beginning of feeling satisfied or happy—most are confused. I cannot remember ever meeting a teenager who could not express to me a list of his or her likes and dislikes, but the skill of discerning *how much* of a good thing is *enough* of a good thing to be satisfied is extremely rare. Teenagers appear able to feel their needs, but not to measure them. The thermostat in their soul reads only "hot" or "cold." This puts them at a huge disadvantage in making healthy choices or developing a moral and spiritual life.

The ability to delay gratification or to build relationships rooted in empathy is based on being able to measure progress in small pieces and to find those incomplete pieces acceptable, pleasing, and sources of joy. Students who have been conditioned by eager-to-celebrate adults to seek spectacular endings rather than stable and fruitful daily practices in their endeavors lack the ability to value the pieces of the whole. These teens are unskilled at enjoying some of what will be the major and never-complete projects of adult life, such as marriage, career, or child-rearing. When the behaviors of adults model that satisfaction is equated with affirmation, and when adults and mentors delay affirmation until final outcomes, it is obvious that teenagers will have a hard time feeling affirmed for anything that is incomplete or ongoing. But the strength to endure and develop skills in life and in love at any age relies on the ability to appreciate the incremental development of skills and strengths.

One reason students have such a hard time delaying gratification is that they lack the ability to judge any amount of incremental growth or productivity short of winning or finishing as *enough* for the hour, the day, or the week. If all the affirmation and love for and within the adolescent comes only at the end of an endeavor, how can any moment in the middle of a challenge bring "enough" of either? You will never find "enough" love among none. Parenting and mentoring that delays affirmation results in needy teenagers who are too desperate to waste their time looking for "enough" of anything in an empty hand. It is no wonder that teenagers have little use for the measurement of "enough." But as long as this skill of learning to love the pieces as well as the whole lies beyond their ability, so too will the joy and satisfaction that fuels self-discovery and confidence lie outside their experience. If few things a teenager does are "enough" for the watching adults around them, few things they do or seek for themselves will feel like "enough" either. The use or lack of use of the word or concept of "enough" in a teenager is a quick way to find out whether or not that teenager is receiving enough of what his or her soul needs in the areas of unconditional love and acceptance. To put it bluntly, students who understand how to measure "enough" of any human experience are students who are receiving enough love and acceptance from the influential adults in their lives.

Skill Four:
THE ABILITY TO FORGIVE

> *"How can you forgive what you can still remember?"*

I had never spoken to a teenager so deeply sympathetic and wise about her recently divorced parents. She was calm and articulate about her father's infidelity: "Yeah, he got lost. He was needy and he went searching I guess. He was selfish, but his father was the same way. None of us helped him though, really. We were the ones who left him alone. And then he walked away." And how did she feel about her mother? "A kind person, but she needs to learn to express what she wants. She's faithful to everybody. So faithful... can you be too faithful to others? I wish she were as faithful to her own ideas and desires. She was a victim long before my dad cheated on her."

And yet this young woman was young enough to hate divorce with an irrational force, despite her maturity in understanding the dynamics of her own family. She said repeatedly that she "understood" why it happened, but that she could never "forgive" what happened. Even three years after the divorce, while she was a very successful college student, I asked her if she had come to think differently about the end of her parents' marriage. She admitted to still being irrationally angry with her parents, asking me, "How can you forgive what you can still remember?"

I have thought a lot about this student over the years. She stands as a clear example that even the most intelligent and mature teenager, capable of rare levels of analysis and understanding of adults, can still get stuck in her own healing and growth by an inability to forgive. For her, forgiveness is nothing more than a form of forgetting.

The skills of the adolescent soul mentioned in this chapter so far do not stand alone. They are like ingredients that have substance and taste in their own right, but also pieces that bake together into creations greater and more powerful than the simple sum of the parts. The fourth skill we now consider, the ability to forgive, relies on the upward spiral of spiritual skill development already discussed in the first three skills. All these skills work together and build up the moral and spiritual self of the teenager. You cannot develop any skill or habit without the ability to delay gratification. No other skill can be fully developed without this one. From this skill grows all others. If you can delay gratification, you can accept failure along the way of any journey because you can inoculate immediate pain with eventual gratification. This skill allows a person to avoid being paralyzed by fear of failure or failure itself.

You cannot develop a habit of empathy unless you are able to invest the time in relationships that allows you to grow in your knowledge of the shared lives we lead. Meaningful, authentic, and lasting relationships are impossible without delaying gratification. And relationships are the ground and the grammar of empathetic living. One cannot delay gratification for very long or nurture empathetic connections without the ability to set and celebrate boundaries that allow for feelings of incremental accomplishment.

The ability to say "enough" and feel satisfied with that boundary is essential to making meaning and deriving pleasure in the pieces of our larger endeavors. Knowing the meaning of "enough" proves that the teenager has been shown and has learned the skill of stretching the joy and affirmation felt at endings backward into every step on the path of any long journey.

This final skill of forgiveness is the hardest of the four mentioned in this chapter and it relies heavily on the other three. It is also the most rare of spiritual skills among teenagers. But like diamonds, its rarity only intensifies its beauty when you see it in a young person. The ability to forgive the world and one's self is rare at any age, but I have found it to be a common habit among the healthiest teenagers I have ever met. Very young children are naturally forgiving, but sadly, many lose this skill during their first decade of life. The ability in a teenager to forgive is more a skill that needs to be resurrected than created.

When it comes to teenagers, the way to teach forgiveness is to preach freedom. The teenagers I know who practice forgiveness are the ones who have figured out that forgiveness is not an end in itself but a means to freedom. All teenagers—all people—seek freedom. And how do you *teach* freedom or truthful and fruitful paths to freedom to teenagers? Here is one simple method I have used. I have found that Franklin Delano Roosevelt's famous "four freedoms" are already familiar to many high school students from their history classes and provide a good start when trying to define freedom to teens. According to FDR's "Four Freedoms Speech" in 1941 and the popular posters Norman Rockwell made famous in the 1940s and long after, the four kinds of freedom that resonate and inspire the human spirit are the freedom to speak, the freedom to worship, the freedom from want, and the freedom from fear. I have never met an adolescent who did not understand and share a longing for these four freedoms to one degree or another.

The spiritual challenge of the parent or mentor of the adolescent soul is to argue that these four freedoms—or any freedom—are only fully achieved by the person who learns to forgive. Among the teenagers I have surveyed over the years, forgiveness for its own sake looks like a self-congratulatory act to them, and parents who preach about forgiveness sound "moralistic" and "judgmental" of those who are not as forgiving. Students resent being told to forgive by other people. Students often see forgiveness as weakness, as giving up on one's commitment to justice or just punishment. Girls and boys over the years have told me that forgiveness is giving up on one's right to be taken seriously. They see the withholding of forgiveness as the last gasp of power for the victim.

I encourage forgiveness by preaching freedom's pleasure and power. I tell stories from my own life, from history, or from current events to demonstrate the freedom that comes from not allowing anger to cloud your judgment, poison your plans, or stunt your creative energies. I use the four freedoms as the fruit of the labor of forgiveness. I explain that holding grudges limits the audience for the expression of your feelings or ideas; that retaining the power to judge warps the experience or expression of your ethics or religion; that withholding forgiveness creates enemies to be feared; and avoiding forgiveness limits the ability to know our true wants by strangling our imagination with the limiting demands of what we deserve. When teenagers come to understand that withholding forgiveness is not power but paralysis—that it stifles rather than preservers freedom—I find they are very open to learning the practice.

The developmental stages of adolescence bring about new powers for the teenage brain. The awakening prefrontal cortex allows for increased levels of awareness of differences, risk assessment, creative connections among individual thoughts, as well as exploding acknowledgment and curiosity for "the other." Teenagers use these emerging powers of analysis and critical thinking to construct new but fragile self-concepts, to choose new affiliations, and to make powerful alliances among peers and philosophies—connections not all of which are healthy but most of which are passionate. At this stage, when the powers of self-determination and self-definition are awakening in the soul of the adolescent, it is difficult for them to forgive the actions of others that they so recently have developed the power to see, measure, and criticize. Forgiveness asks the young soul to show mature wisdom. But the students who learn to forgive rather than ignore or resent the failures of others experience a freedom to reconnect and relate that is the essence of the newest capacities of the adolescent brain. More than ever, the teenage brain and heart want to reach out, to understand, to connect, to be intimate, and to be loved. Forgiveness is a path to all these innate and powerful desires of adolescents. When we teach them to forgive the world for its poverty, cruelty, racism, bullying, and all forms of injustice, we are not teaching them to forget what they see every day but instead we are calling them to love the world beyond what it earns. This is precisely the standard of love that teenagers seek from the world, so the practice and skill of showing this love to the world and to everyone in it is a natural habit that breeds hope for that habit to spread. Young people want to be the people that they long to know. The skill of forgiveness gives them the chance to be the heroes that they seek. It also allows them the freedom to learn from their past without carrying the baggage of grievances about their past. Forgiveness creates more room in the soul of the adolescent to carry more wisdom and gratefulness. Adolescents do not store anger in the soul as efficiently as adults. It easily crowds out all other emotions. In my experience, any lovingly offered suggestion to a teenager about how to replace that anger with freedom is a welcome skill.

In the space of three months in one of my years of teaching, I had two very different seventeen-year-old boys come to talk to me. Both asked me to take the same walk with them to the school parking lot. The request of each was identical. "Do you have a sec? Can I show you something?" And those two very different boys nonetheless followed a nearly identical script on the flight to the parking lot: "Just wait . . . you'll see . . . just wait!"

The first boy who invited me to see his car was an affluent and only child. He often said that he got along very well with his parents "when they were available," although the three lived more like "roommates who shared a common space." The boy was moderately successful in many areas of his life, though tending to laziness and settling too easily for grades that were average and below his potential in most subjects. There was something incomplete about nearly all of his endeavors. He was aware of this but did little to change it.

For his seventeenth birthday, this young man was given a new Volvo. I picked it out immediately with its temporary cardboard license plate as I chased the birthday boy to its parking space in the school lot. He walked me around the outside of the car two or three times to recite "the specs," as he called them. I did not know much about the automotive details he listed and I wondered if he did either. More than anything I was speechless at such a luxurious birthday gift for a teenager.

Despite his mediocre grades or infrequent meeting of adult expectations for his life, he was very bright and quickly ascertained from my quiet reaction that I was perhaps judging his birthday an unworthy occasion to receive a new car. "My parents wanted me to have a safe car," he said somewhat defensively, "and you can't beat a Volvo for that, can you?" Before I could respond, he pushed a remote control tucked in his hand to unlock the car doors. He then jumped into the car and turned the key for me to "experience the sound system." When the engine started up, the music—still on the settings from his drive to school earlier that morning—was so loud it knocked me back in my leather throne. He was embarrassed at the blaring noise and quickly turned the volume down in a motion with his hand so fast I barely saw it happen.

I couldn't help myself: "Do you think speakers with that volume-potential while you drive are part of that 'safe car' goal your parents had in mind?" He smirked. "Don't worry, I'm careful," he lied. After a few more brief sentences, I left him listening to his music as I walked back into the school. With every step I took, I heard and felt the volume of the speakers getting louder and louder.

The second teenager to hang around after class until I noticed him was one of three children, the oldest child of hard-working parents. He was a strong student with high grades and preparing to be an Eagle Scout. He complained occasionally to me about his "annoying" and much younger siblings, though I caught sight of him on more than one occasion enjoying his little brother and sister as he brought them to school events, tying their shoes and zipping their coats. He had a lot of responsibilities at home. He loved community service projects. He was shy about his acne, but confident in his ability to complete tasks. "I know how to get stuff to work," he would admit under his breath whenever helping a teacher or peer work out a technology problem. Both his friends and his teachers said often that he was resourceful, reliable, and mature.

The car we approached was an older Honda littered with new bumper stickers to proclaim all of this boy's passionately held political views. He read newspapers daily and asked adults in his life about their opinions of current events while he eagerly shared his own. I do not know enough about cars to say much more about "the specs" of this used car, but the small amounts of rust above the wheels told me it was at least ten years old.

I asked why he got the car. "It's my birthday this month," he said. He was so excited that he was stuttering half-sentences and nearly rubbing the hair off his head with nervous scalp-scratching with the hand not holding the keys. He was beaming just to be near the car, although he shared with me that he had been driving it for two weeks already. He could not keep his hands off it while he told me everything about the engine, the brake system, and the "aerodynamic design."

Together we sat down on the curb. His voice was full and proud of his newly acquired wisdom about driving. "You gotta be careful around here... people drive like maniacs." I nodded. "You can't use cheap oil with an old car like this, even though it's tempting to go Jiffy Lube. And it'll need new tires in about a year. I read that you should change them every thirty thousand miles. Who knew?" I nodded again. He reached forward and slowly ran his fingers along the tread of the tire. "So I'm going try to drive as little as possible because I won't be able to afford new tires for a long time."

For the first time I took my eyes off the car and turned my head toward him. "*You* have to buy the tires?"

"I said it was my car, didn't I?" He didn't take his eyes off the tire.

"Oh yeah," I apologized. "Yeah. You did say that. So, *you* bought this car?"

He smiled. "Well, like, two-thirds of it. That's what my dad said I had to do: 'two-thirds.' My birthday present from my parents was the last third . . . and the insurance for a year. But the insurance is only a gift for *this* year, and, well, I have to pay for some of that too. I only get half my allowance now for doing the same stuff at home. The other half goes toward the insurance. When I graduate, I'll have to pay all that by myself, but I did some research online and I think I can get cheaper insurance than my parents have now. I'll also have a good driving record then, for sure, so that will also bring down the cost. It's all good."

I sat quietly during the details of the birthday deal. I was impressed. "That sounds like a pretty complicated deal." He didn't flinch: "Life is complicated." I raised my eyebrows and nodded in agreement with this mature observation. I reached over and patted him on the back. "Happy birthday, my friend. You'll never forget this one, will you?" He smiled, and then sighed like a happy but middle-aged man. "Just hope those gas prices don't spike. Half an allowance doesn't buy you many miles."

I knew this boy's family well enough to know that they could have bought their son a used car without all these financial machinations. He could have had the car, kept his allowance, and, like many young people, not even known that cars must be insured in this country. But his parents had a goal that was obvious. They did not want to give him a toy. They wanted to give him a gift that would be a source of both happiness and maturity. This is the same boy who once told me that he asked for a puppy for Christmas when he was ten and got one. But "the deal" with getting his dog was that he would have to walk that dog at least once a day until he went off to college. He wrote a contract promising to do his part, signed it in red crayon, and left it out with the cookies for Santa. From what I knew, his upbringing was a seamless garment of this kind of skills training; no gift left unused in the journey toward maturity and discipline.

Two boys. Two gifts. One boy got a toy. The other boy got a tool. One boy was given a gift that he did not earn and did not have the skills to own or use responsibly. The other boy was given a gift that he had not only earned, but that he was also asked to invest in. As a result, the old car might take that boy farther than any new Volvo because it might pull him toward greater maturity and dig in him a well of skills to generate his own happiness for life.

Toys generate dependence on those who provide them. Tools generate independence for those who receive them. Toys train teens to receive; tools compel them to grow. The new Volvo will teach one boy to drive back to his parents for the next new toy. Since the gift came with no sacrifice on his part, it is hard to imagine how he will ever give up any desires he has to speed, waste gas, or blast music. The Volvo was not the result of delaying gratification, so why should its use ever be an exercise of delayed gratification? Having a free new car means he is also now continually owned by his parents in order to maintain it. The boy who saved for four years to pay his "two-thirds" will instead be pulled by that car and its needs into his own future with the confidence and pride of earning and maintaining what you have. Possessing luxurious unearned gifts morphs quickly into a sense of privilege, not pride.

I am sure that the parents who gave the new car told themselves and their son that this car was an opportunity to show responsibility. Whenever parents spend their resources on phones, computers, or any other big-ticket items for their wage-less teens, they justify the gifts as paths toward adulthood and discipline. I am sure the new car came with many unheard lectures about rules and expectations. But gifts like these only give teens opportunities to practice and strengthen skills they already have—skills in making choices and accepting consequences that are nurtured (or not) by parents from early childhood years. The lesson I have learned about when to give or withhold gifts to teens is that gifts should be given *after* skills in discipline and responsibility are proven, not prior to demonstrating such skills in vain hopes to inspire skill development with unearned presents. Giving gifts to those who are not yet skilled to use them wisely and therefore joyfully is not generosity, but distraction.

Similarly, many parents with whom I work state that they are "very connected" with their kids on a daily, if not hourly, basis because of the cell phones and laptops that they provide. I see what they mean. My students send emails and text messages to their parents throughout the day. But when I ask my students what they are saying in all those lightning-fast finger typing sessions, they share openly that most of these "conversations" are, at best, requests for money, rides, or schedule changes, and at worst, arguments, excuses, or lies that create a false sense of adult connection or parental awareness of their child's daily life. When I ask the parents why their children have cell phones as early as elementary school, the nearly universal answer revolves around safety: "We gave them a phone so that we can reach them and they can reach us when they need to." I am not against safety. But statistically, the greatest threats to the lives and health of young people are not things that can be avoided or escaped through text messages or crisis-reporting calls. The greatest threats to young people are high-risk behaviors. And the greatest enabling forces to poor decisions that I have ever witnessed are handheld phones and round-the-clock and unsupervised Internet access. The ability to communicate constantly with every person you know or have ever known in the palm of your hand without anyone else knowing that you are doing it presents a far greater threat than anything a phone call will save you from.

The answer is not to remove phones and computers from the lives of our children. Arguably they would not be prepared for the wired world ahead of them if we turned Luddite fears into parenting paradigms. However, the problems with unrestricted cell phones, unlimited texting plans, and Internet access serve as perfect examples of the pitfalls of giving toys and not tools to our kids. I can speak for myself as an adult who often prefers giving kids freedom instead of giving them formation. Giving our kids technological or financial capacity without taking the time to fully form their skills to handle freedom takes a lot longer than handing them a new device and articulating a mouthful of rules. Skills are not the fruit of hope; they are the product of structure.

The desire to bond with our adolescent children can also take the form of over-rewarding any positive behavior or apparently open conversation with the most valuable forms of gifts: money, increased access to cars, and increased privacy or "freedom." A significant number of students say that they funded their addictions to pot, alcohol, or drugs with money their own parents gave them as rewards for good behavior, good grades, or for going out to movies or restaurants. I have had dozens of parents tell me over the years that they would prefer to give their children money than withhold it in order to provide the means for their child to "have a safe evening of eating out or going to a movie." Meanwhile, their students are asking to be dropped off at movie theatres that they never enter. These students Google the reviews on their cell phone Internet connections and are therefore ready to discuss the film they did not see when they meet up with their parents at the theaters a few hours later. The stream of cash given to students to buy "safe fun" becomes the funding source for drugs or alcohol, for the student to whom it is given or for their needy friends.

Young men and women state constantly that the experience of being given money—or any large or ongoing gift like a new car or frequent vacations or club memberships—that they did not earn created a destructive fault line in their characters and made them into people ripe for addictions of any kind. As one former student who became addicted to cocaine said to me, "You just can't have something given to you for nothing, from middle school through college, and not develop an addiction to those gifts, to other people's money, and to other people's stuff." He went on, "I got to college and realized I couldn't get or make any of the things that felt basic to me. It's like I was wired to have more money, cars, and stuff than I could ever provide for myself. I was addicted to my parents' giving long before I ever developed an addiction to anything on my own."

That is why we adults have to be intentional about the separation between our own capacity to consume and that of our children; between our social habits and theirs, between our money and theirs. It is a characteristic of this generation of youth to be closer to their parents than those of Generation X or Baby Boomers. The result is that this generation of parents is more likely to invite their children to share their wealth, travel, or technology. Whereas past generations of young people experienced joy or self-discovery in rebellion from their parents, this generation of teens is addicted to the spending power and giving habits of their parents. More and more I see parents in every economic bracket shopping with their kids as a form of connection, giving them high-priced clothing brands that are made and priced for high-paid adults, or taking their kids and their peers to restaurants far too expensive for any teenager to afford on their own. All parents want to be a part of their teenager's life. But more and more this generation of parents is achieving this goal by dragging the child into their own lives, consumption habits, and social cliques.

Wise parents want their children to experience pleasure as a reward for their own work. This is the way to teach skills and encourage maturity, rather than to subsidize a child's participation in the social or economic habits of the parent. It is so tempting to buy intimacy by dangling toys before our teens. In the short run, it may create a breeze of intimacy between parent and child. But in the long run, we send these children out into the world sure only of what they want, with no skills beyond the ability to come back to us for more.

 *Chapter Six*

LIGHTHOUSES AND PIRATES

Skills for Parents and Mentors

"High school feels a lot like playing Follow the Leader every day. Some days I feel like there are too many leaders saying conflicting things and I want to quit the game. Other days I feel ready to play but I can't find any leader at all."

I had never seen a lighthouse for real before I walked into one in Maine. Like millions of bookstore-browsing Americans, I saw lighthouses only on Edward Hopper greeting cards, countless calendars of New England, or cheap mouse pads. But one summer, friends took me to see the Portland Head lighthouse at Cape Elizabeth, Maine. While there, I eavesdropped on a tour and overheard a fact that brought lighthouses to life for me: "Lighthouses are not monuments," said the tour guide. "They are living lights that save lives." At that moment the lighthouse began to work in my mind as both my image and my goal for being a spiritual mentor to adolescents.

Teenagers are like young sailors setting out on their first solo voyage, full of desires, hopes, and fears. At this age they are ready and eager to follow their pulsing desires to date, to drive, to try out, to quit, to cheat, to drink, to gossip, to enlist, to lie, to kiss, or to try anything that will give them an experience of choice and consequence. This is the age of commitment, a time when they want to feel their freedom. Those of us adults who love teenagers and want the safest and happiest voyage for them have to decide how we will practice love and exercise our responsibilities as parents and teachers from the shore. We have to learn to manage the grief we feel over passing on from our central role in their safety and sense of discovery during childhood into a more distantly supportive role in their adolescence. Parents who do not let go of their patterns of parenting with young children will wind up with adolescents who act more like young children than young adults. They need us to adjust to their burgeoning maturity with the appropriate levels of direction and distance. If we do not find a way to give them room to grow, they won't. If we give them too much freedom and lack of direction, they can become anxious or confused, deferring to the ever-present levers of teenager life like peer pressure or the power of advertising. So we have to learn to manage our fears as we witness our children mature into a world that we know through our own experiences will bring pain and suffering. It is incredibly difficult but necessary to chart a course for how we will love and support our children as we watch them set off beyond our reach.

Those of us who are raising and teaching teenagers can learn a lot about methods of mentoring from lighthouses. Lighthouses reach lives from a distance; they do not guide by *going*, but instead beckon by *being*. They clarify reality rather than attempt to create it or control it. Lighthouses do not take sides; rather, they allow others to see truths without attacking or defending what they reveal. Lighthouses preach by reach. And most importantly, lighthouses do not exist to pull travelers toward their own positions. Journeys would end in tragedy if any lighthouse pulled a ship toward itself. Lighthouses and where they stand are not the end points for travelers who see them and follow them; lighthouses are not tractor beams. Lighthouses that save lives do so by serving the sailor in safe pursuit of his or her own destination.

I also learned from my lighthouse tour that according to sailors, the potency of a lighthouse is measured not in its height, structure, or position, but rather in how far from the shore the light can be seen. Lighthouses are not valuable for their beauty but for their beam. Moreover, the single determining factor in how far a light can reach out to sea is the complexity and cleanliness of the rows of lenses that surround the single bulb. Can there be a more potent image for the spiritual mentor of an adolescent than a light that emanates only as powerfully as the number of angles it has on the world and the pristine quality of its vision? Can there be a more encouraging truth for mentors than to realize that teens value a mentor not for her outward beauty but for the clarity of her beam of light?

It is a myth that only young teachers or youthful parents can reach the young, or that only adults who drown themselves in youth culture are popular with teenagers. Young people trust and follow mentors who are lighthouses, not neon signs: adults with the self-possession to know where they stand and who stay there against cultural pressures. The adults whom my students trust and love are light-keepers who do not prevent the young from being the navigators of their mysterious and often inscrutable spiritual and social lives. Great spiritual directors of adolescents are not pirates; they do not hijack the freedom of the adolescent. Too many teachers, coaches, and parents try to steer conversations toward their own convictions, insert their own vocabulary into discussions, or seek dialogue with adolescents that only reaffirms their own assumptions.

Like so many ships, every young person in our life is potentially going to a different place, by a different path. Helpful spiritual light-keepers are often unaware of where each soul is ultimately heading or from where each has come in his or her journey. A strong and mature mentor does not have to know or agree with the past and future choices and worldviews of the teenager. What any sailor needs from a lighthouse is help, not confiscation of the mission. In spiritual direction I think it is my role to stand firm on the ground of my own convictions with students who are on their own journeys to and from places that might be a complete mystery to me. It is not my vocation to draw those young people to my views or get them to swerve in a direction that is meaningful to me. I want the young people in my life to receive from me the freedom to become navigators of their dreams, largely by creating sacred spaces of reflection in conversation that help them see where their spiritual lives have been, where they are now, and where they might go.

A senior boy I once taught loved zombies. Recalling his utter fascination with the concept of zombies, I am convinced that wherever he is in his adult life, he is still thinking about them. This student had seen dozens, perhaps hundreds of movies about them, played endless hours of zombie video games, and could not do a creative writing assignment for me without referring to zombies in some way. As soon as I noticed this light-hearted fixation, I started a nearly daily process of asking him questions about zombies. Although he did not identify himself as religious in any way, I recognized his consuming interest—some might say his obsession—with zombies as thoroughly religious in its constancy and sense of community with other zombie fanatics he knew in person or from the Internet. I did not try to alter his interest or talk him out of his beliefs about zombies; I just listened to him share his passion for what he believed. I asked about the ethics of his beliefs, the kind of communities he wanted to live and learn in, the role of technology in his activities about zombies, and what vocations he might consider in his future.

While talking about ghosts, we also shared our fears of other things. While talking about his beliefs and questions about spells and witchcraft, we also discussed our hopes for medicine and education. I still do not know what a zombie is, exactly. But in putting aside my skepticism, along with my abhorrence of the whole idea of a zombie, I made room in conversations for this zombie-loving student to share with me his loves and frustrations for countless other realities in his life. I never fought against what he loved, nor did I pretend to love it. What I showed him was my excitement that he obviously knew how to love something passionately and loyally. I acknowledged the amount of information he had amassed and the commitment such expertise requires. When he saw the light of my pride for his personal project to master the concept of zombies, our conversations eventually became deeper, longer, and took up many more topics, to the point that we rarely discussed zombies at all.

We will all run across dozens of beliefs and hobbies of teenagers that will strike us as odd, silly, upsetting, or confusing.

We must try not to hijack their passions, but let them show us where they have been, where they are, and where they are going before we weigh in on their choice of path. When they tell us of destructive choices they have made or are making, we enter the conversation as the passionate advocate for their health and happiness, not the promoter of our morality or the conduit of our fears. But above all we stay on the shore by reminding them always that our desire is not that they agree with us, but that they find the safest and truest path toward adulthood. A light-hearted phrase I use often with teenagers is, "I want you to get where you are going with peace . . . and in one piece."

No metaphor is perfect, and this metaphor of being a lighthouse has to be used with care. Lighthouses are fixed sources of light, after all, but the concept should never be used to justify never changing one's mind. Young people need adults in their lives who are lifelong learners, confident enough to change their worldviews when new information challenges old convictions or traditions. The story of the Cape Hatteras lighthouse is a helpful guide. Built in 1870, this historic lighthouse was in serious trouble: the very shoreline that existed when it was built had seriously eroded and the lighthouse was in danger of being swallowed by the water. Then, in an ambitious community effort, the lighthouse was raised, placed on metal tracks rubbed with soap, and pushed inland to a safer location. Enough care and thought was put into the relocation that the foundation was just as strong in the new location as it had been for two centuries in the old.

Although young people need adults to stand firm in their beliefs and standards, adolescents also need to know that there are times—however few—in our lives as adults when we have to admit that the shores of our past understandings have moved and that we are willing to change our stance. I have seen young people follow adult leaders passionately when those leaders admit their mistakes, tell stories of times when their views changed, and celebrate the power of learning new ideas and expanding their circles of friends. Lighthouses that move too often will weaken their foundations and be unable to project light. But the teens I know want adults in their lives who can accept that our multicultural society poses new challenges with every click of a mouse.

On the hot-button issues such as race relations, gay rights, or immigration, our teens want to know if we are willing to admit that shores of certainty can change. Do we have the courage to change in order to renew the power of our light?

So what are the skills of the light-keeper? How do we avoid being pirate parents and mentors? How do we know when to stand firm and when to move our lighthouse? And how do we add new frames to the lenses through which we view the world? I believe that for adults to nurture the skills of light-keeping we need to take hold of three skills: the ability to find a message, a method, and a metaphor.

FIND A MESSAGE

Years ago, two boys in my ethics class asked me to speak at their upcoming Eagle Scout badge ceremony to be held locally. Both boys had finished all their tests and projects and, as close friends, wanted to have the ceremony together. I was honored that they asked me to do it. "We want you to tell everybody what it all *means.*" In the silent wake of that last word, you could hear a badge drop. My face broke into a wide smile and I dared not hesitate. "I am honored! I'd love to!" They breathed out loudly, "Thanks! Our moms will call you soon. Cool! Thanks!"

This conversation with the two boys was actually the second time I had thought deeply about the Boy Scouts of America that year. The Supreme Court had recently handed down a decision addressing whether or not openly gay men or boys could be a part of the organization. The High Court overturned a lower court's ruling against the Scouts that called exclusion based on sexual orientation unjust discrimination and illegal. The Scouts appealed to the Supreme Court on the basis that they were a private organization and they won the right they sought to discriminate against members based on sexual orientation. I heard many colleagues share their views of the Supreme Court decision in the weeks that followed it. The media had also been temporarily obsessed with the case and what it meant for the cause of gay rights in the country. Schools were common places for such debates because—as anyone who works with young people knows—the issue of gay rights is clearly unfolding as the primary civil rights question of this generation.

I had doubted that the boys who were preparing to receive their Eagle Scout badges that year had strong feelings on the subject. When the issue came up in one of our ethics classes later that month, I sat quietly while their peers asked the soon-to-be Eagle Scout boys what they thought about the rights of gays in scouting. The scouts had no opinion: it was as if they'd never heard of the issue. The national frenzy appeared miles away from their personal accomplishment and raw excitement to complete their path to the pinnacle of scouting. I assume few boys involved in scouting across the country that year were as interested as the adults in the controversy; in my experience, youth are more often apathetic props than actual players in such public debates about "what is good for our children."

As the date of the ceremony approached, I watched how the rising temperature of the national discourse about discrimination in scouting was affecting the *adults* in America. More and more public schools and other organizations receiving federal funds announced bans on Boy Scout use of their facilities with every passing week in the wake of the Supreme Court ruling. Our nation was, as with so many difficult moral issues, taking sides. I spent hours at the computer trying to get information about becoming an Eagle Scout so that I could learn enough to say what it all "means," but too often the sites I visited were consumed with the present controversy rather than the rich history of the Boy Scouts.

The boys had put such confidence in me, having heard me give inspirational speeches to young people on many meaningful occasions, but in truth I was completely ignorant as to what they had accomplished or how. I learned a lot in three weeks and developed enormous respect for the positive and powerful influence that scouting has on young boys and girls. Of course, I was also growing in my understanding and conviction that this culture of potent mentoring explains why so many Americans care deeply about how this organization defines a "morally straight life." I came to understand the stakes being driven into the hearts on either side of the civil rights issue of who can and cannot take the Scout's Honor pledge.

When I talked about my impending role as a speaker at a scouting event with liberal friends, more than one asked how I could "in good conscience" have anything to do with an organization that discriminated against any group of people. On the other hand, my conservative friends were jealous of my opportunity to "support the Scouts" in this most recent chapter of the culture wars. Everyone agreed that because I was a teacher, I had a "moral responsibility to affirm moral principles" in whatever I said. I tried to voice my conviction with friends that students need the gift of our unqualified support at rites of passage, not self-serving political agendas packaged into their memorable moments. Everyone felt this answer to be a cop-out. Others said my decision to stay out of the political issues made for "a lost opportunity" to add moral content or encouragement toward character in a teachable moment.

But I could not get the proud faces of my two students out of my mind. Their focus on the individual joy and meaning of the event was my model and set my agenda. I promised myself to speak *to the boys* about the good they had accomplished and not touch the eight-hundred-pound political guerilla that had been present at any gathering of the Boy Scouts that season.

I share this event because I feel that it exemplifies a situation in which many adults find themselves. So often it is our deep desire to be given a chance to speak to young people in their meaningful moments and to reach out to them in a compassionate and wise way that helps them grow. But when these moments arrive it is not always clear *how* we should share the love and learning we have. How important are our convictions in the face of the budding convictions of the teenager? How do we keep our fears out of the energy of the conversations? How do we avoid sounding judgmental without erring on the side of relativism? How do we honor the ideas of the teenager without abdicating our responsibilities to be the adult in the situation? Whether our kids ask us about drugs, sex, college, money, or the meaning of life, it can be very stressful to write an authentic, appropriate, but no less adult script that can speak liberating truths to the soul of the adolescent. Whether preaching in pulpits, speaking at podiums, conversing at dinner tables, or driving in carpools, every adult has been in these potentially mentoring moments.

Like so many parents and teachers who search the World Wide Web for words of guidance in communicating to young people, I was still left with the personal decision of what message I wanted to send about what it means to reach a rite of passage. I could not figure out what else to say to the boys beyond "congratulations," though I knew they wanted so much more than that from me. The challenge was to find a message about what it means to be a part of an organization, to adopt its moral code, and to follow its defined path to adulthood and honor. Scouting is a clearly defined moral community, but it is also a meritocracy like so many in this country. Banners and badges mark and rank the completion of challenges according to rules of participation and service. The hierarchy is present and powerful. The question that haunted me in participating in such a serious event as the crowning moment in the life of a scout was the same question I worry about whenever adults give profound public rewards to children and teens for achievement. How do we celebrate a child's accomplishment while simultaneously sending the life-saving message that achievement is not necessary to be a person of worth to the world? That is, how do we hang badges on kids without branding their hearts with the dark idea that love is the reward of their achievement? How do we celebrate a rise to the top yet still affirm the universal dignity and worth of all people? I have read many articles and books on parenting and teaching that dictate adults be honest and authentic with young people, but this prescription to speak the truth is easier to make than to take.

What was needed, as far as I was concerned, was a message about meaning beyond meritocracy—not an easy agenda to import into a subculture whose metric for morality is "merit badges." My research with teenagers has made it clear, however, that the message they are hungry to hear at moments of accomplishment is that achievement itself does not earn love or dignity. When we respond to their accomplishments with pride and showers of love, we have to be very careful. We have to be clear about exactly what is and what is not "achieved" when our kids win or perform better than others. The words from adolescents show me that in most cases, adult-led celebrations with trophies and titles lead teens to think that only in winning do they earn affirmation or establish their value.

On the spot, I decided to talk about *The Wizard of Oz.* My challenge was to mark a glorious achievement, but also to do so in a way that did not honor any particular achievement over the self-knowledge gained by both boys. I wanted to honor the journey more than the badge. And when it comes to depicting the meaning of journeys that begin with desire and end with glory, the message of *The Wizard of Oz* is one of the best.

You might be thinking that it was silly for me to talk of Scarecrows, Lions, and Tin Men on that serious day, with all the flags and badges and honored guests. Maybe it would have been silly— if no one in that room had ever been a confused intellectual, uncertain about their emotions or paralyzed by their fears. We have all been a scarecrow, a tin man, and a lion in our journeys. My message to those two boys was that their future would be a journey during which they might question the powers of their minds and bodies, as well as question the existence of any real courage or love anywhere in their souls. And here enters the Wizard. You know from the tale that he is not what everyone thought he was. He was just a man. But you also know, after he confesses his lie and changes his ways, he becomes a pretty good teacher. In fact, the transformed Wizard is a great role model for anyone. Though he was just an ordinary man, he brought an extraordinary message to this troop of travelers.

You see the travelers came to the Wizard to get things that they thought they did not have already. We all go to such wizards. We go to politicians, to doctors, to huge bookstores, to scout masters, to movies, to coffee houses, to churches. We all search for wizards to give us what we think we do not have. But we learn from the story that the power of the Wizard is only in his ability to bear witness to gifts already present and to acknowledge those gifts with signs of affirmation, like the diploma, the hanging heart, and the crown. It was the journey that *proved*—not created—their gifts.

As I stood at that podium I wanted those boys to know that the wizards of our world do not make intelligence or love or bravery. These gifts exist in all people. The only difference is that some of us take the journeys that prove to us what we have and strengthen the power of our gifts, and some of us stay home and spend our days wondering whether we are gifted at all. Some teenagers spend years wondering if they are worth the love of those around them. On that day, I shared the message that those boys did not simply come upon gifts like bravery, as if they were lost on the side of the road. In service to others, they found the bravery that resides in every soul.

At the end of the ceremony, I marched out behind the flag bearers, scout marchers, and newly branded Eagles. When I reached the back of the room, the highest-ranking adult scout walked up to me. He looked upon every young scout in the room with the love of a proud father, while the badges on every inch of his shirt told the story of his love of scouting. His gaze at me was kind but suspicious. "Thank you for supporting our scouts," he said while giving a firm and lingering handshake. I smiled and thanked him for his ongoing support of so many of the young men in our community. I wondered what he really thought of my speech, with its message of the mistake of making any hierarchy into a holy thing or of mistaking any wizards for the Creator. Before he let go of my hand he saved me from wondering any longer. "I see why the boys wanted you. You've got a way with words, ma'am. I guess we all have our wands, right?"

FIND A METHOD

I suspect few people had ever heard of Kevin Kelly outside a small world of tech-savvy folks before Malcolm Gladwell mentioned him in his 2007 bestseller *Blink*. Gladwell introduced his millions of readers to this maverick who had been a pioneer practitioner and philosopher of technology for decades. Back in 1984 before he created and became executive editor of *Wired* magazine, Kelly wrote an obscure but magisterial book entitled *Out of Control: The New Biology of Machines, Social Systems, and the Economic World.* He set out to take note of the principles of biological evolution and apply those principles to artificial machines and all manmade systems. Throughout his five-hundred-page tome, Kelly names this method of mimicking evolution in manmade endeavors "bio-logic," and argues that the secret to structuring any successful system lies in obeying bio-logic.

From the overwhelming complexity of Kelly's technical and multidisciplinary meditations on the future bio-logical relationship between man and machines, Gladwell pulls out one observation and uses it to support his argument in *Blink:* Humans are most creative and productive when they are free to follow their instincts rather than imposed rules. The gem from Kelly is that there is a simple but mighty principle in the evolutionary process that can be adapted by any person or project and that aims for constant growth and boundless improvement. If we want to succeed, all we have to do is learn to be "in command and out of control."

When I hear students speak of their longings for love and their innate desire to discover the depths of who they are and to be supported in this inner journey, I return again and again to the riddle that our kids need two apparently contradictory things from us: freedom and restraint. Despite the fact that one of the only human occupations not mentioned in the prolific writings of Kevin Kelly is parenting and that Gladwell did not set out to write a chapter or book on parenting *per se,* Kelly's simple phrase "in command and out of control" is the best description of a healthy method of parenting and mentoring of young people that I have heard in a long time. Gladwell eagerly appropriates and popularizes Kelly's phrase because it suggests a solution to the riddle for any leader/follower or parent/child relationship: How can more than one person be in control of a life? Must the authority of the leader mean the atrophy of the follower's freedom? Teens cannot develop their own skills unless we let them try and fail and learn. But how do we fulfill our responsibilities as mature adults who actively assist our kids without stifling their freedom?

According to Kevin Kelly, natural selection breeds the greatest diversity and superior adaptation because it preserves freedom *and* obeys natural laws. Evolution is a process in which all organisms are locked into a universe where the laws of nature rule, but simultaneously each organism is allowed the freedom to adapt to those laws in its own way. Gravity and other natural laws govern the world; no organism can change the laws of life. But the laws of nature are "out of control" when it comes to the individual choices and changes any individual organism makes when faced with the restraints of natural laws. The result is a world teaming with lives that are all improvising responses to the fixed laws in their own way, developing new ideas, new capacities, and eventually, new species and entirely new communities of life. If natural laws controlled both the rules *and* the responses to the rules, there might be conformity in life, but there would be no creativity, no diversity, and no progress. There would be no selection and evolution, but only replication. Natural selection rewards innovation, diversity, ingenuity, and hard work.

Gladwell borrows this evolutionary principle of "in command and out of control" from Kelly when he discusses methods of successful leadership in *Blink*. He argues that military commanders or leaders of companies or communities should practice "in command and out of control" leadership in order to awaken and encourage the freedom and energy of followers. This style of leadership requires the leader to be fully "in command" of the group through the creation and constant restatement of the mission goals of the group or organization. The leader must resist the temptation to suggest or require any particular *method* for achieving the goals of the mission by a member or members of the organization. The idea is that if the leader is crystal clear about the mission or the goal of the group—and if that leader insists upon keeping every member of the group accountable throughout the implementation of the mission—then members will be free to achieve the goals in an explosion of individually crafted and diverse methods. Allowing each member the freedom to respond to the command of the leader with his or her own methods leaves the leader "in command and out of control." Great leaders must learn to manage the inevitable stress and fear that comes with leading an "out of control" organization.

If there is one phrase that captures the dynamic parenting style that produces morally and spiritually skillful teens, it is "in command and out of control." There are two parts to this kind of parenting. First, the parents must lay down the laws of the family and hold every person (including themselves) accountable to that mission, no matter what. This is what it means to be fully in command. They have to be willing at any moment to stop an activity—however inconvenient the interruption might be—if the mission of the family (to be respectful, to attend church, to tell the truth, to share) is compromised. Some families never make it to this stage. We all witness parents in public whose children clearly violate their family rules in airports, restaurants, or school functions, but it is clear that the parent makes a decision that it would be too much of a disruption to "stop the world" and fully address the violation. Many of us know what it would look like to hold members of the family firmly accountable, but we are unwilling to sacrifice other goals to address misbehavior. Likewise, our children often watch adults violate rules and see that there is no command structure that corrects the obvious violation. For example, they see adults smoking despite the cancer risk, speeding in their cars, parking illegally, or speaking unkindly about in-laws. Rather than address the violation and correct it immediately, we often breeze by these mission-failures in order to meet lesser goals, like being punctual for an appointment, not missing a family event, or "not causing a scene." But our children notice this lack of command of the family values and it teaches them to expect, tolerate, or spread chaos.

What does it look like for a parent to be out of command? I was sitting in a school bus full of my ninth-grade basketball players at one of my first teaching jobs. We were idling in the school parking lot, waiting for a mother to arrive with her daughter's uniform. We were ready to leave when the young girl opened the sports bag that her mother packed for her that morning only to discover the white uniform shirt instead of the necessary red one. The girl screamed in anger at her mother, picked up a cell phone, and half cried/half yelled at her mother to drive to the school "immediately" and correct the problem. Did she call her mother a "bitch," or did I only imagine it?

The family lived only fifteen minutes from school, so I agreed to hold the bus and wait. During this waiting time, the girl got off the bus and paced back and forth around the parking lot. Her anger turned her whole face red and she stared out into space with young but vengeful blue eyes. Her mother finally sped into the parking lot and pulled right up to her daughter's outstretched arm. I only saw the mother's hand reaching out with the red shirt, which the teenager snatched up. This motion shocked me, but not as much as what happened next—she flung the white shirt right into the driver's seat of her mother's car, all the while yelling words like "Stupid!" through the window. I was a young teacher and coach only a few years older than the screaming teenager, but I was old enough to know that I had seen enough.

I got out of the bus and walked swiftly toward the girl. But the mother's car drove away too fast for me to engage them both and I was left with an angry fourteen-year-old girl looking suspiciously at me. I asked a simple question. "Did you just throw that shirt at your mother?" She paused, clearly embarrassed that I had taken note of the exchange. She covered herself with a lie: "Mom said, 'Just throw it in,' so I did. She's in a hurry, you know." And then the girl walked away from me with a wicked smile for her quick recovery and self-defense. I had no immediate strategy to punish her. Her mother's quick exit robbed all of us of the opportunity to address the tantrum in the moment.

The next morning I was at my desk well before school started, grading papers in the quiet stillness of a high school before sunrise. I looked up to see the mother of the tantrum student. She was dressed for work. She was alone. She stepped only two feet into the room, stopped, and said quietly, "I came to apologize. I know my daughter was inappropriate yesterday and I know you probably wanted me to do something about it." My first thought was, "Why isn't your daughter in here apologizing to both of us?"

"She said that you told her to throw the shirt in the car," I said as I stood up and took a step or two closer to her.

"No, I did not. Nor would I tell her to throw anything: that is not how our family operates. She just threw it and stormed off. I knew there was no point in saying anything else because you were all in a hurry."

"I got out of the bus to show you that we did not have to go anywhere quickly and that dealing with the outburst was worth all the time we needed."

She stood quietly. Then, "I know. I know that's why you got out. I know you think I should have done more."

"I did not know exactly what to do. But yes, I did feel like we needed to do something from the moment she called you."

She paused again. "I would have told her to stop yelling, but I know she would not have listened. I would have told her to get into my car and that she was not going to the game because of her tantrum. But she would not have listened to me and that would not have helped anyone. I decided to just wait and deal with it at home."

"So what happened when she got home?"

"Well, she's grounded next weekend. She's already going to the winter dance this weekend and then with us to New York on Sunday, so we'll have to wait for the following weekend to punish her."

It is tempting but imprecise to say that this mother let the situation get "out of control." It is more accurate, using Kevin Kelley's language, to say that she was "out of command." The daughter clearly felt like the commander of the situation, from the moment she noticed the uniform problem and called to scream at her mother and order her to drive to school. The daughter treated her mother with disrespect and abuse, and did it with style and a smirk—evidence of a prior pattern of disrespecting her mother, and doing so in public. The mother made the decision to put off the corrections for a more convenient time. She allowed the daughter's desire to leave for the game dictate when the correction would occur. And worse, when the belated correction was delivered, its consequence was put off for a week in order that lesser values, such as inessential social plans, remained intact. When a parent is out of command, the child can take control.

The second brave stage of "in command and out of control" parenting is without question harder than the first. Parents have to resist the temptation to institute or micromanage the methods their children adopt to meet the mission of the family, or the mission of schooling, sports, or other occupations of childhood. Parents have to learn to sit back and watch their children succeed or fail on their own powers in order to digest lasting lessons. Parents have to learn to be "out of control." I meet very few parents who are able to practice this kind of discipline when the stakes are high for their children in sports, academics, or other paths of performance. The prior example of the basketball player who had a tempter tantrum toward her mother is an example of this. Rather than being in command of the values in the family by modeling and insisting on appropriate patterns of talking and being respectful at all times, the mother was clearly pouring her efforts instead into trying to take control of the details of the daughter's life on the day of the basketball game. Why was the mother packing the sports bag and choosing which uniform to pack in the first place? This was a smart and creative girl who was certainly old enough to pack a bag for day. Yet on that day or any other, the mother had decided that controlling the packing of her daughter's things was the quickest and safest way to support her teenager. The result, however, was not helping the young person succeed through skill development, but rather supporting a lack of skills and thereby creating dependence on parental involvement. Whenever children strike out at their parents it is usually the result of resentment once the teenager realizes their dependence on parents. Parenting by being overly involved in control rather than in establishing command leads to teenagers that will undoubtedly strike out at that control whenever something goes wrong. The goal of "out of control" parenting is that the child or teen learns to create possibilities and meet responsibilities on their own and in a way that plants lasting skills. Teens also learn to take direct personal responsibility for mistakes because there is no one else to blame. That mother put herself in the line of fire.

Many parents handle the role of being "in command" very well. I see their students in my classes or on my teams carrying day-planners, reciting directions from adults, and able to articulate moral goals for their endeavors. However, many parents let this command carry over into control, demanding and rewarding conformity to their own parental plans or projects for the child's day rather than letting the child structure his or her freedom in pursuit of the goal for the weekend, the season, or the year. This is the parent who calls the teacher in addition to telling the child to talk to the teacher, who sets up the appointments that a teenager could arrange (but might not) on their own, or who brings the child to events to ensure that he or she is not late. This might be a parent "in command," but it is also a parent who is "in control." As a result, the parent is on the gas pedal constantly, allowing the child to ease off the clutch and become complacent and unskilled in his or her own life. When parents are in control and in command, how can their children learn to balance command or control of their own lives? Then adolescent anxieties increase:

> *I don't know if I can do well on my own.*
> *I don't know how to pull things off.*
> *I don't know how to keep my success going.*
> *I'm afraid college will prove that I can't do anything on my*
> *own.*

Intelligent teens figure out very quickly in high school that they lack the skills they see in peers or adults. The greater freedom they are given in high school and eventually in college or independent life only raises anxieties because their inability to use it fruitfully creates downward cycles of failure and guilt. The children of parents who insisted on command *and* control have been trained to know what they want and to know what others want for them, but they also know deep inside that they are untrained to be successful on their own. They have been trained to dream, but not to build.

A memorable and brilliant example of the wisdom of "in command and out of control" as a parenting style is found in Stephen Covey's classic, *The Seven Habits of Highly Effective People.* Covey tells of his attempt to give his preteen son a chance to take greater responsibility for chores around the family home by inviting his son to accept responsibility for the care of the front lawn. His father gave the son only one clear command: "Keep the lawn green and clean." Covey did not prescribe any method for keeping the lawn "green and clean," though he did offer to help the son at any time. Covey stated that there would be a periodic review of the lawn to see whether or not it was "green and clean," but that a daily or weekly schedule for lawn care would be entirely up to the son to develop and uphold. Covey set up the perfect situation: he was in command as the creator and upholder of the "green and clean" mission; he was also intentionally "out of control" of how or whether his son was going to meet that mission.

In the first month of the summer, the son failed. The lawn was brown and unkempt. Covey watched the failure happen one day at a time. But he did not intervene. At the scheduled review, he took the son on a walk around the property and the remorseful boy wept at his failure. The two sat down and discussed the problems and possible solutions. The son had learned a hard lesson but changed his ways and finished the summer with a lawn that was brilliantly green and clean.

What I have always loved about this story is the public nature of the boy's first failures and the particular temptation Covey must have felt to rescue his own lawn. Covey and his wife had taken good care of the grass before they handed this chore to their son's young and inexperienced hands. I am sure they were somewhat embarrassed to witness the appearance of their property, and perhaps its perceived value, sink in full view of the neighborhood. There was probably some anxiety that the grass would brown to a point of no return, causing financial repercussions that the young son could not have seen coming. The illustration brings into full view the stress involved for parents who try to practice "in command and out of control" parenting. But the lasting reward of allowing children and teens to set their own course and learn from any mistakes is a young adult with self-taught skills to last a lifetime.

So often parents who are aware of the liabilities of micromanaging their children continue to justify their actions by saying to me things like, "Well, we know she is not doing her part now, but let's just get her into college first because that is too important a thing to leave in teenage hands." When I read the exploding binge drinking statistics—well over 40 percent of students report binge drinking at colleges and universities across the country every year—I am reminded how shortsighted the "get them into college first and then worry about skill development later" method really is. Students smart enough to go to college are smart enough to realize whose work ethic got them there. This is a very upsetting fact to students who are finally at college and now have to perform at the parent-enabled level on their own. Is it any wonder why alcohol becomes a medication for managing that enormous stress?

The widespread stated anxieties of our teenagers about their future and their ability to thrive in the world testify to the fact that we are not giving them the skills or letting them develop the esteem that comes from skills. We are not willing to let the lawns of our children's public lives go brown—whether those lawns are academic transcripts, athletic opportunities, or part-time jobs. We too often practice the dysfunctional rescuing that replaces their faltering efforts with our own. The result is that we adults get better at school projects, making teams, taking tests, meeting deadlines, and writing college essays. And we send our kids into the world lectured enough to know we expect them to succeed, but rescued enough to doubt that they can.

FIND A METAPHOR

My mother called me recently and confessed that she had made her first expensive purchase from the twenty-four-hour television channel called Home Shopping Network. She had seen a product that was "absolutely amazing" and she had ordered one for me as a gift. She wouldn't tell me what it was, but said it would "change my life." She did not often speak this way about material things, so I waited eagerly for the delivery. Within a week, I opened my gift parcel and found a small but high-end Global Positioning System (aka GPS) to place on the dashboard of my car.

Not long afterward I saw a five-minute spot on Home Shopping Network for the same product and finally understood why my mother called that toll free number. The salesman sung his pitch. "My friends, you no longer need to be afraid on the road!

You no longer need to worry about how you will handle a crisis. In fact, you won't run out of gas anymore wondering where the stations are. You won't worry that you can't find a hospital. You won't fear driving in the dark. You'll simply NEVER be lost—ever again." It was the most intensely spiritual pitch for a material object I had heard in a while. By the time this altar call was over, I understood why any parent worthy of the name would have a hard time saying no to buying a GPS for their child. Apparently, someone had created a piece of technology that addressed nearly every primal fear a parent has on the day their child gets behind the wheel.

My first trip with the GPS was probably the most dangerous road trip I've taken in a long time. It is extremely difficult to transition from decades of driving on your own to watching and listening to the new super-brainy passenger chatting on your dashboard. It felt crowded to have two drivers in my brain, each with fixed ideas. I took a handful of rides to familiar places where I work and shop. In most cases, the GPS agreed with my chosen routes and her spoken directions matched my desired route. But occasionally, as I would take my secret side roads and violate the computer directions, I would receive the silent treatment from my GPS. Then the passive-aggressive announcement: "Recalculating." This was her method (I could have chosen a male voice, but I didn't) of letting me know that I could have my way for a moment or two, but that she was planning to catch up to my ideas and reestablish herself as the leader the trip.

Within our first twenty minutes together, I found the most important function on my GPS: the mute button. It's been months now and I can't even remember her voice. I don't mind a picture of where I am going. Nor do I mind the suggestions on turns when I occasionally embark on new destinations. I have always loved pulling over and consulting maps, but I don't like the constant voice of directions while en route because it distracts me from making actual decisions. I have also noticed that when I follow the directions of the GPS, I arrive at my destination with little or no lasting knowledge of the route I took. Getting lost takes time but it also can breed knowledge of the area that can be applied later on. With the GPS, I arrive as clueless as if I had never taken a trip.

Seeing the GPS on my dashboard now reminds me of the first piece of technology that occupied that spot in my first car. When I first learned to drive our family's preowned Nissan, there was a small black plastic compass glued to the dashboard. I don't remember if we put it there or if it came from the previous owner. It stood about two inches high, with a round compass floating in liquid. It bobbled around constantly from the moment the car started up. I knew nothing of how to read a compass and I suspect no one else in my family had any idea how to use it either. So although it hinted at helpfulness, our inability to use that compass rendered this jittery low-tech navigation system about as useful as a pair of fuzzy dice hanging from the mirror. Technology has come a long way from that plastic device of two decades ago, but that old compass is a clear symbol of a timeless truth of parenting. Every parent and mentor of adolescents has a choice to make: Will we be a compass or a GPS?

The usefulness of a GPS is that it tells you exactly what to do. But in my case, the voiced directions keep me from learning about where I am and where I am going; the only skill I learn and practice is obedience. I do not learn to consult maps, recognize landmarks, or memorize the landscape. I am too focused on listening to the voice and following the personalized map provided for me to add my own voice to my thoughts. This is what Kevin Kelly would call "in command and in control" guidance. Anyone using a GPS knows that feeling of increasing anxiety once you have decided to shut off your own ideas and follow the digital leader. Following street after street of computerized directions, you become more and more dependent on the machine-mind who now is the only one who knows (you hope) what to do next. You might be approaching your destination, but you are moving further and further away from your own knowledge and abilities with every turn. To find your goal, you have to lose yourself.

When parents act like a GPS, they nurture children in the addiction to directions. Destinations are usually reached, but the only skill a child practices is obedience. When we as parents overassert our abilities in the lives of our children to help them succeed, we want to call it "love" or "creating opportunities." But the sad fact is that when we become the pilots, we become the pirates.

The young people I meet with resilience, creativity, and self-confidence are those whose parents were more of a compass in their preteen and teen lives. A compass points you in a certain direction, but that is all. It leads you toward a goal but says nothing of the route to that place—you are on your own to find the path. One also needs to learn how to use a compass. There are skills involved. A traveler must do some navigational work before setting out on a journey with a compass. The ongoing information coming from this timeless tool is only meaningful if you know where your journey started and where your destination is in comparison to your current location. You need perspective, memory, and patience.

The powerful truth for parents about a compass is that it does not offer *directions,* but a *direction.* This is the secret to becoming an "in command and out of control" parent or mentor. In an age of inexhaustible information coming at us and at our children, parents and mentors have to resist the temptation to serve their children by piling on endless and ultimately disabling directions for success. What they need from us is direction, not more directions. They need moral, spiritual, and emotional direction, which means talking about goals, beliefs, hope, and faith. They need us to take command as role models, to live lives worthy of the children who are watching us so closely to see if we believe what we say. They need us to articulate the missions of our lives and how we choose them. They need us to hold our families and ourselves accountable when we experience mission-challenges or mission-failures. They need us to stand firm and shine light, not to swim manic rescue missions to take the helm of their freedom and steal from them the wisdom that comes from running aground from time to time. Most of all, adolescents need us to overrule our fears about letting them steer their ship. In my experience, it is only love that is powerful enough to disable the fears we have for our kids. We have to love their freedom so much—and long for the lifelong skills that grow from freedom—that we refuse to calm our fears by overcontrolling their lives. I muted the GPS voice once I realized that it was silencing my own mind. Our adolescents can do the same to us.

 *Conclusion*

SOULS AT SEA

"The shadow beneath that bright leaf over there...."

We walked out of the suburban church together one evening after I finished delivering a lecture on how to help teenagers avoid high-risk behaviors. She had questions of her own, but these were not questions she wanted her fellow church members or even her family members to hear. She asked if she could walk me to my car and talk along the way. "Of course."

She began to talk about her two children—identical twin daughters who were, at that point, juniors in high school. "They were so cute as children! We always dressed them the same. They were best friends until middle school. I think middle school was when they started growing apart."

We stood at my car for an hour as she described the tale of the two sisters. One excelled in athletics from middle school into high school, even as her academic courses got harder and harder. She had a part-time job—"Her bosses always say she's their best worker." This daughter had a serious boyfriend for three years, walked the family dog every night without being asked, and sang in the church choir. "We worry she takes on too much. She definitely exercises too much. But she is such a pleasure to have around. I think she enjoys being around my husband and me as much as we enjoy being around her. She loves to please. She knows we love her and that we are so proud of her."

And then there was the second daughter. In middle school she pulled away from her sister and made her own group of friends. "We didn't know those kids she hung out with. They were like fringe kids. We thought they were trouble from the start." The mother then poured forth a painful narrative about how the second daughter "got lost" and had "become a stranger" to her own family. "I think she's tried everything. She's experimented with every dangerous thing, as far as we know." This mother had been called into school for intense meetings about everything from stealing to drinking, smoking, and even periods of cutting and other self-destructive behaviors. This second daughter dyed her hair different colors, had a habit of yelling at home and cursing at her parents. "We don't know what to do. Punishment doesn't work. She does not respect us. I don't know if she even likes us. We love her so much. But we have run out of ideas on how to reach her. We don't talk anymore except to fight. We are afraid for her health and safety every single day. She is playing with fire and she knows it." The mother's eyes filled with tears. "I can't believe how different my daughters are. How could two girls who share so much grow into completely different teenagers?"

When she had reached this question in her narrative, she stopped and we both stood in silence. There were clearly hours more she could speak, but suddenly she was quiet. She had told me her name at the beginning of this intense exchange, but that was an hour before and I had forgotten. I did the only thing that felt appropriate. I reached over and hugged her. She was awkward, but did not resist the embrace. When her face emerged off my shoulder I said the first thing that came to my mind. "You know, your daughters don't sound all that different to me." Her eyes immediately squinted, as if she wondered whether or not I had been listening to her at all. "Well, that's not what anyone else thinks," she said without any emotion. But I smiled, slowly and broadly. She appeared ready and eager to feel the peace that was on my face about her family. But she clearly did not understand how.

I then began to speak about the similarities between the two girls, despite how different the manifestations were in their actions. I talked about what I believe to be the longings of any adolescent soul: the need to connect with others; the need to find, define, and follow one's own purpose and passions; the need to adopt projects that spark and stretch one's skills; and the need to find out what the world thinks of the teenager. I said that both these girls were following those desires and trying to meet those universal needs of their souls.

Both girls had succeeded at finding opportunities to bond with peers—one through committed dating and the other through equally intimate though group-based exhilarating behaviors like drinking, smoking pot, or stealing. Both girls were learning to navigate sources of intimacy, according to the longings of the adolescent soul to make promises, keep secrets, and experiment with the power of love. They both developed public practices that let everyone else know their habits and bravery, their strengths and their ethic—one in athletic uniforms or choir robes, the other in tattered jean jackets and blue hair. And both were developing high-risk habits to mask or even medicate the naturally high levels of anxiety that accompany this development stage—one spending too much time exercising and the other spending too much time sneaking around school to smoke or experiment with drugs. Both girls seemed driven to show the world that they do not wear the same parent-prescribed clothes as their sister anymore.

And most importantly for this mother, I shared my conviction that both girls found a way to answer one of the most crucial questions for any adolescent: What do the adults in my life *really* think of me? It is amazing to see the dangerous distances our children will travel away from us into high-risk behaviors to try and answer this question of worth and love. The mother's own words made clear to me the only real difference between these girls. The A-student overachiever "knows how much we love her and that we are so proud of her," while the acting-out sister "has become a stranger to us . . . we don't even talk anymore."

There is never any one answer for families in crisis. But I believe in my heart that the needs of the adolescent soul are universal. I have become convinced of this reality by hearing the confessions of teenagers about their shared experiences of the soul, as well as by seeing the apparently different but actually similar ways that teenagers are looking for meaning and unconditional love. I congratulated the mother for raising two clearly creative and passionate girls who, in their own ways, cared enough about their own lives to find ways to take control of their passions and define their lives. But I also encouraged her to do the only thing a parent can do with teenagers who are acting out: find ways to show more love than fear, find moments to articulate more acceptance than frustration, and seize every opportunity to offer the clearest and most constant answer to the teenager's search for parental love. "Relieve both your daughters of the burden of wondering what you *really* think." Sometimes we use all our words, in the heat of frustration, to share our fears and judgment. We cannot assume that our teens are aware of anything else in our hearts. And I added my opinion that she should not ignore the obvious love-hungry and approval-seeking habits of her A-student daughter. "There's nothing wrong with running on treadmills. Just be vigilant about whether or not your child is running from fears of failure." Unconditional love is the only sustainable fuel for the unconditional needs of the soul of the adolescent.

There was an awards ceremony at school that Friday and all my students were dressed up in ties and jackets, or dresses. I noticed a boy in my classroom who was not known to spend any time on his clothing. He was competitive in academics and athletics, but he devoted little attention to matching socks or keeping his shoelaces tied. Because I knew his apathy for dressing up, I could not help but notice his perfectly tied bow tie that Friday morning. It even had a slight imperfect tilt, proving that it was a real bow tie.

I walked right up to him. "So when did you learn to tie a bow tie?" The class smiled as his proud face beamed. "An hour ago." I then noticed that all his close friends in the room also had on bow ties, though theirs were nowhere near as well tied. Clearly, this group of friends had chosen bow ties to show the school how fun and bonded was their clique of friends. "So who taught you to do that this morning? It looks great."

Without pausing, he blurted out, "I Googled it. Turns out YouTube had over ten thousand videos on how to do it. Who knew? The video I clicked on was actually in some foreign language, but who cares, right? I just watched the guy do it. Two minutes. Done." He was barely touching his tie, so as not to mess it up. He stuck his neck out and rotated his upper body in slow swings back and forth so that everyone in the class could see the fruit of his Internet consultation.

I had asked the boy who tied his tie in hopes to learn something about his household. Did he have an older brother who took the time to explain the art of the bow tie? Was a grandparent or other relative visiting or living in the house? Did his father or mother take a few moments before going to work to teach such a fun lesson? It did not occur to me until I asked that the teaching moment was not with a living person in his home or in his life, but rather with a video in a mysterious language, recorded in a faraway country at an unknown time. The boy explained that he had the perfect knot before he even left his bedroom. "You have a computer in your room?" I asked, as I tried to imagine this predawn tie lesson on the World Wide Web. "Yeah, but I didn't use it. I get YouTube on my phone."

Our teenagers have powerful emotional and spiritual needs that are God-given magnets pulling them toward meaningful, productive, and joyful adult lives. But I am reminded every day that teenagers will find a way—however helpful or hurtful—to meet their needs with or without our help. If a student can learn to tie a bow tie on his phone, what else can he learn to do in the privacy of his room without even getting out of bed? Did he consult the phone because there were no adults in his life who would have given him the time of teaching a lesson over breakfast? Does his family even have breakfast?

The reality of the Internet is that our teenagers will have company, friends, teachers, and other influential voices that we will never know. And teenagers who are naturally hungry for connection will utilize the technologies we offer. There is positive and powerful information on the Internet that improves lives every day, and it is futile to condemn its role in twenty-first-century America. I am not concerned that my student went to the Internet to learn how to do something meaningful to him. But I am concerned if he went searching because there were no adults around him who are present, nonanxious, and affirming of his needs and passions. We calm our fears for the fate of our young people only and effectively through equipping them with the skills necessary to navigate the billions of other souls online.

A young bright senior girl who had been my student in multiple classes over her years of high school brought me one of the biggest shocks I have experienced in a conversation with a teenager. Her innocence was something I noticed and enjoyed every day. She was blonde, petite, usually smiling—even giggling—throughout the day. She liked stickers, loved her pets, and did not engage in the popular habits of gossip or complaining. She seemed genuinely happy and sure of herself.

To this day I do not know what I said in class to spark her desire to share a secret with me. I was talking about "organized religion" and shared a few national statistics about the popularity of traditional religions and atheism among teenagers. She said nothing during class, but came up to me as her peers left the room. "If I show you something, will you still respect me?" She had to ask twice, since her voice was naturally soft and lost in the noise of exiting peers. When I finally heard her request I froze. "Still respect you? Well, I think so. I can't think of many things you could say that would cause me to lose respect for you." At this point, only she and her best friend were still in the class. I was getting very curious. "What do you want to show me?" She exchanged a glance with her best friend, who nodded as if to say he thought I was safe. She turned around and lifted her pink shirt. And there tattooed across her lower back in dark black letters was the sentence: "God is the weak man's salvation." I was stunned. This was a girl who loved Disney movies, making her own music, and talking about her pet turtles. She turned back around to face me. "Do you still respect me?" she said shyly, blinking her childlike blue eyes. "I certainly respect your boldness," I said. "I'm an atheist," she offered up as she gathered her schoolbooks and prepared to leave. "Wait," I said as I walked toward her. "Where did you get that phrase from?" She walked toward the door and then stopped. "I found it on the Internet. I kind of liked it."

"You 'kind of' liked it?!" I said in a very loving but no less animated voice to try and bring the appropriate level of gravity to her tattoo. "You had it carved into your back. You must really believe in atheism." I rarely meet teenagers who use this word to describe their beliefs. And this was definitely the first teenager I knew well who had tattooed such a belief into her skin.

She looked hard into my eyes, measuring my interest. "My mother doesn't know. She would die." I kept her gaze. "Why would your mother die if she knew?" She sighed in a way I had never heard before. She took a deep breath and by the moment she seemed to be getting older and older. "Well, my mother is a totally conservative Christian. She hates my beliefs. I hate hers. If she saw what I wrote on my back she would be so sad she would die."

"So why did you write it then?" I asked. She paused, then said confidently, "It's not about her. I wrote it because it's my life and my body. And, because it's true. I am not my mother." Her innocent smile returned with that explanation. Then her ponytail flipped as she turned and walked away. I was left watching the little plastic gnome with blue hair hanging from her book bag bounce up and down as she skipped off to her next class. Given no room in her relationship with her mother to feel ownership and pride for her own life and beliefs, she used her very flesh to make room for the sharing of her truths. The soul of the adolescent will find expression, no matter where the canvas or what the price.

Her definition of the soul was scribbled out in less than a minute. She came in while others were already writing, picked up the question sheet with an apologetic smile, and held out her leftover lunch as if to ask for permission to finish it. She was the first to

finish writing out her definition of the soul and jumped up to hand in her sheet with a simple, mouth-full smile. She handed it back so quickly that I assumed her sheet was blank. While she returned to her seat to finish her lunch and while her peers were still writing, I looked down at what she had written under my question "What is your definition of the soul?" In pink marker, she wrote:

> The shadow beneath that bright leaf over there
> Splinters in a fence ready to break
> The horizon on a foggy day
> The silver lining on a raindrop too small to see
> The electrons released in your brain by a big sigh
>
> Your second instinct after reconsidering
> All the questions you ask
> Hunger
> Chaotic thought processes
> When you are surprised by your physical senses
>
> It is something lonely
> It is something we make when we think
> It is something that yearns to hear music
> It is something that can respond to song and
>   that is like water
> We continuously distill it to try to make it clearer
> We can't know if it is a part of us.

When I looked up at her, I saw a teenager tapping her foot to some internal music with her mouth full of junk food and her eyes wandering around the room looking for something to look at. One shoelace was untied and her hair was a mess. She could have been any age from eight to twenty-eight. I looked down at the words again, thinking that if I hadn't seen the page blank a moment ago, I would not have believed they could have come from her. There is no doubt that this young woman's mind is unique in its poetic force and artistic skill, but nonetheless I was reminded then as now that our young people carry around in them so much reflection and conviction about their interior life. All we have to do is ask.